Tiptoeing Through TULIP
A Crash Course Comparison of Classical Arminianism and Calvinism

Nicholas Campbell

Copyright © 2023 Nicholas Campbell
Published by Christ is the Cure
Boerne, Texas

All rights reserved. No part of this book may be reproduced in any form on by an electronic or mechanical means, including information storage and retrieval systems, without permission in writing from the publisher, except by a reviewer who may quote brief passages in a review.

Illustrations copyright © 2023 by Christ is the Cure
Cover Design by Rebekah Campbell

ISBN [Print]: 979-8-9885721-0-7
ISBN [ebook]: 979-8-9885721-1-4

Unless otherwise indicated, all scripture quotations are from The ESV ® Bible (The Holy Bible, English Standard Version ®), copyright © 2001 by Crossway, a publishing ministry of Good News Publishers. Used by Permission. All rights reserved. Confessions are modified from Philip Schaff, *The Creeds of Christendom*, Bibliotheca symbolica ecclesiae universalis in 3 volumes, New York: Harper Longmans, 1919, Public Domain.

Quotes taken from *Why I Am Not an Arminian* by Robert A. Peterson and Michael D. Williams. Copyright (c) 2004 by Robert A. Peterson and Michael D. Williams. Used by permission of InterVarsity Press, P.O. Box 1400, Downers Grove, IL 60515, USA. www.ivpress.com. Quotes taken from *40 Questions About Arminianism* © Copyright 2022 by Matthew Pinson. Published by Kregel Publications, Grand Rapids, MI. Used by permission of the publisher. All rights reserved. Quotes taken from *40 Questions about Calvinism* © Copyright 2019 by Shawn Wright. Published by Kregel Publications, Grand Rapids, MI. Used by permission of the publisher. All rights reserved. Quotes taken from *Holman Illustrated Bible Dictionary* © Copyright 2003, ed. Brand, Draper, England. Published by B&H Publishing Group, Nashville, TN. Used by permission of the publisher. All rights reserved.

To my wife, family, and patrons

Contents

Introduction	ix

1. **HISTORICAL POINTS OF INTEREST** — 1
   - Pre-Pelagianism — 2
   - Pelagianism — 5
   - Detour on Monergism and Synergism — 9
   - Semi-Pelagianism — 12
   - Reformation Era History — 19
   - Luther in Brief — 19
   - Beza and Arminius — 21

2. **TOTAL DEPRAVITY** — 31
   - Original Sin Introduced — 32
   - Original Guilt — 36
   - Calvinism on Original Guilt — 40
   - Arminianism on Original Guilt — 44
   - The Corruption of Man — 47
   - Arminianism on Total Depravity — 53
   - Calvinism on Total Depravity — 59
   - Summary — 62

3. **THE HUMAN WILL** — 65
   - The Spectrum on the Human Will in Ancient Judaism — 68
   - Arminians and Libertarian Free Will — 71
   - Arminians and Sovereignty — 75
   - Arminians and Foreknowledge — 80
   - Calvinists and Compatibilism — 82
   - Calvinists and Foreknowledge — 95
   - Summary — 97

4. THE DOCTRINE OF GRACE	99
Grace broadly defined	100
Arminianism and Prevenient Grace	101
Arminianism and Resistible Grace	106
Arminianism and Irresistible Grace	108
Conclusion on Arminianism and Grace	111
Calvinism and Grace	113
Calvinism and Irresistible Grace	113
General vs. Effectual Calling	118
Calvinism and Resistible Grace	123
The Two Wills of God	128
Conclusion on Calvinism and Grace	133
Summary	134
5. CONVERSION AND REGENERATION	135
Summary	141
6. PREDESTINATION AND ELECTION	143
What is Election?	144
What is Predestination?	148
Election and Predestination in Arminianism	149
Romans 8:28-30 and Arminianism	154
Ephesians and Arminianism	157
Romans 9 and Arminianism	159
Election and Predestination in Calvinism	165
Romans 8:28-30 and Calvinism	171
Ephesians and Calvinism	174
Romans 9 and Calvinism	175
A brief interjection on Romans 9	181
Summary	185
7. THE ATONEMENT: ITS EXTENT AND OTHERWISE	187
Introduction: Misconceptions and Agreements	187
Arminians on the Atonement	191
Calvinists on the Atonement	194
Summary	199

8. PERSEVERANCE OF THE SAINTS 201
   Calvinism on Eternal Security 202
   Arminianism on Eternal Security 209
   Summary 213

9. CONCLUSION 215

   Appendix A: What does "Reformed" mean? 219
   Appendix B: Council of Orange 223
   Appendix C: Arminian Articles of 1610 227
   Appendix D: The Canons of Dort 231
   Appendix E: Additional Resources 261
   Notes 265
   Select Bibliography 277
   Index 281

Introduction

The topic of Calvinism vs. Arminianism is often a polarizing and heated debate. It's easy to find arguments for or against either side online, and in many of these discussions, you'll find less than fruitful interactions. The conversations are tense, and strong convictions exist on both sides of the aisle. Individuals further complicate matters when they treat the debate as a gospel issue (i.e., to hold one or the other position is to be a heretic!). Others will dismiss the discussion as irrelevant and needlessly divisive.

In response to this, it must be said, first and foremost, that Calvinists and Arminians are brothers and sisters in Christ. Secondly, there needs to be some thought regarding one's position on this topic. The topic matters. You cannot avoid the reality that "predestination" and "election" appear in your Bible. The subject *will* impact how you view the Christian experience. It will affect how you understand your conversion, growth, and continu-

Introduction

ance in the faith. Where you land on this topic will inform and likely answer questions such as, "Can I lose my salvation?" Furthermore, it will affect how you pray for others and even participate in apologetics!

The student of scripture cannot ignore these topics. Perhaps you are thinking, "This is how I understand it," or "I'm content with it all being a mystery," but we must understand these issues have been debated so much because they are about Biblical concepts.

Many excellent works have been published on the discussions of Calvinism and Arminianism. However, unless you draw from sources on both sides of the debate, you'll begin to develop caricatures of each position. This short book will assist you by providing a crash course summary of the similarities and differences between Classical Arminianism and Calvinism. The goal of this volume is simple: to help eliminate some strawmen, which are misrepresentations of a position, and open the floor for better discussions. I also hope to encourage the practice of stopping to ask questions in discussions. As we'll see, many of the common issues in these conversations can be solved this way!

This book is not meant to be a persuasive argument for either side nor will it give you every detail of the two positions. Instead, it will touch on key points you'll need to consider - many of which will highlight how the debates are often framed around the wrong issues. For example, believing the discussion is ultimately about predestination vs. free will is overly simplistic.

As we will see, Calvinists believe in free will but

Introduction

qualify it differently than non-Calvinists. Likewise, Arminians believe in predestination! It is a mistake to think that Calvinism equals predestination and Arminianism equals free will. The right questions are more complex. How do Arminians understand free will and predestination? How do Calvinists understand these topics? Other fundamental misconceptions will also be addressed, such as the idea that Classical Arminianism doesn't believe in total depravity, the idea that Calvinism is fatalism, or that Augustine invented compatibilism.

I hope this book can give you a bird's eye view into the continuity and discontinuity between Calvinism and Classical Arminianism. In doing so, we'll find that many myths are dispelled about the systems and ideas, such as a possible Calvinism-Arminianism hybrid or the idea that it is not either/or but rather "both/and." Additionally, as we'll see, Calvinism and Arminianism are not necessarily opposites but have common ground at some points.

It needs to be stated that this volume limits its discussion on Arminianism to Classical Arminianism (though I will often refer to it as Arminianism throughout this book). This is further limited to a particular form of Classical Arminianism that seeks to re-stress the 17th-century, reformed roots of Jacob Arminius. This is not 'modern' or 'pop' Arminianism but the earliest form of Arminianism (which does have continuity to various groups today). The same could be said about Calvinism in this volume, but Calvinists have the advantage of being more uniform on most points.

I would also like to address the use of labels for

Introduction

Calvinism and Arminianism. Why do we need to be in a specific camp or apply these labels? In short, nobody *needs* to. The labels should not be so central to our identity that they are subversive to our identity in Christ. Instead, they should be understood as a means of quickly understanding where somebody falls on issues found in scripture. Just as the titles of Baptist or Paedobaptist are not something that supplants Christ but rather inform us of whether or not one holds to infant baptism, these labels are not problematic when kept in proper perspective. We must also recognize that there is a usefulness to such labels on more serious issues! For example, consider a Trinitarian and a Jehovah's Witness. If we remove their designations, we'd have a mixture of heresy in orthodoxy and couldn't identify who is who. Furthermore, we can say, "Let's not use the labels" until the cows come home, but they will continue to be used regardless by those around us, so we might as well correctly define, understand, and engage with them.

This book will begin with some historical points of interest relevant to current discussions. The historical points in this book have been selected based on conversations I've seen most often. The goal is to lay out some basic terms, people, and events to better inform the reader when observing discussions on Calvinism and Arminianism. From here, we will speak to those doctrines found in TULIP (the acronym for Calvinist doctrines), but not in the traditional order—the reasons why will become evident as we work our way through them.

Finally, a necessary disclaimer for this volume is that Reformed[1] and Arminian theology are more than their

Introduction

five points. This will be demonstrated briefly in our chapter on the human will in particular, but it will not adequately express the richness and depth of each tradition. With this all stated, we can move into the historical points of interest.

Chapter 1
Historical Points of Interest

When speaking on the subject of soteriological systems such as Calvinism and Arminianism, we cannot do so without beginning with some historical discussion. This historical discussion will focus briefly on the pre-Pelagian era, then the Pelagian and semi-Pelagian controversies. Defining semi-Pelagianism becomes a point of contention in modern discussions, making such a preliminary discussion necessary. While many may think that the historical theology surrounding these topics is unimportant, they can clear up strawmen on both sides of the debate and help inform where we fall on particular concepts.

Here, some key terms and ideas will be introduced, then more fully discussed later. While I will try to define all relevant terms, some points may be assumed. Thus, some brief independent searches may be necessary, or chapters may need to be revisited by individuals after they have read further in the volume.

Pre Pelagianism

During the era prior to the Pelagian controversy in the 400s (AD), early Christian writers had a diverse expression of soteriology, which are the doctrines related to salvation. Instead of concentrating on how salvation worked, they were predominately focused on Christology[1] due to various heresies arising during their period.

Christians typically quote the New Testament without much exposition on the subjects we are currently focusing on, such as predestination. While there are many instances where no explanation is provided in texts regarding foreknowledge and predestination, there are some references to election being based on foreseen faith or obedience. Furthermore, Christians spoke much of man's free will, usually in the context of moral responsibility and accountability. Much of the early discussion also pushed back against the concept of fate by emphasizing free will. While such discussions on free will were frequent to uphold human responsibility and right living, we know little about how early Christians understood the dynamic of free will in light of divine sovereignty. Put another way, we know they held to these concepts, but we don't know how they understood them concerning one another. This is evident in the fact that theologians would debate these topics in years to come. Those debates were not occurring amongst Christians at this time.

We find the atonement being spoken of in universal terms - that Christ died for all men. Yet, while the atonement was spoken of in these universal terms, it was still regarded as limited in its application. They held to the idea that one must have faith to have the atonement count on their behalf. Many Christian writers believed that Christ died for the whole world. Some writers would speak of the atonement's effects on the entire created order – sometimes crediting the atonement for the deterioration of paganism/polytheism. Christian writers assumed that man was sinful from birth and needed salvation, but to what extent they viewed this corruption, we do not know.

Early in the church, the belief is found that God gives regeneration, or the new birth, through baptism (the details of which are also debated) and that the gospel was a message of grace. The controversies on soteriology (concerning Pelagianism) broke out after Christians were granted freedom from previous persecutions. Yet the dust settled on the Pelagian/semi-Pelagian disputes fairly quickly, as further Christological questions dominated Christendom's mind. Robert Peterson and Michael Williams, in "Why I am Not an Arminian," summarize as follows,

> "While affirming the necessity of grace for salvation, early Christian theological reflection tended to be highly moralistic and even legalistic, emphasizing a view of the Christian life that focused more on conduct—often expressed as rigorous prescription—rather than grace, faith or forgiveness. In comparison to Augustine's monergistic doctrine of grace, the teachings of the apos-

tolic fathers tended toward a synergistic view of redemption. For them, salvation is the result of a working together of divine grace and human agency. Human beings are fallen such that they need divine help, but that help cooperates with our own striving toward God and the moral life."[2]

Historical Points of Interest

Pelagianism

Moving into the soteriological controversies, we begin by looking at Pelagius. Pelagius was a British monk who was at odds against Augustine in the 5th century.[3] Current scholarship is debating how much of the polemics against Pelagius were correct in their assessments of Pelagius' actual teachings. Some have put forward that Pelagius suffered much due to misrepresentations over and against the traditional understanding that Pelagius taught what he was charged with. Here we will follow the traditional articulation while keeping in mind that Pelagius may not have taught these doctrines himself, though the doctrines would be condemned by Christians regardless.[4]

According to traditional articulation, Pelagius taught that there was no change in the nature of man from the fall of Adam. Contrary to Augustine, Pelagius denied that man inherited any corruption or guilt from Adam's sin in the garden. The concept of passed-on guilt and corruption is typically denoted as original sin. To put it another way, original sin is commonly conceived as the notion that all humans are born with a corrupt nature and the guilt of Adam's transgression in the garden because of his disobedience. In some views, original sin is defined as original corruption without original guilt. This view holds that men inherit the corruption of Adam, which is a sinful nature but not Adam's guilt. Instead, they are only guilty of the sins they commit. How Adam passed on corruption and/or guilt is articulated in various ways. Yet, Christendom has recognized original corruption as fundamental Christian theology – all men are born sinful except the incarnate Son of God.[5] The primary point to focus upon is the notion that Pelagius put forward: man is neither guilty nor corrupt because of Adam.

From here, Pelagius taught that humans were born in moral uprightness and could merit salvation without any grace or aid of grace from God. These alleged teachings of Pelagius were condemned ecumenically at the council of Ephesus in AD 431. The notion that man is without corruption from sin and can merit salvation by his own freedom, apart from God's grace, regardless of whether or not Pelagius and the Pelagians held to such a teaching, was ecumenically out of the question.

To better understand the situation, we can look at the man on the other side of Pelagius - Augustine. He argued that when Adam disobeyed in the garden, man became enslaved to sin, so he now seeks sin and sees sin as good. Instead of being inclined to follow God's will, man's desires align with the devil to seek after sin. Augustine posits that man cannot escape sinning after the fall of Adam and described humanity as "not able not to sin."[6] Just as well, Adam and Eve lost their freedom and moral integrity while also gaining death when they disobeyed God's directive. Adam had lost true freedom and life and became enslaved to the powers of sin and death. Adam had been corrupted, along with his children, which is all of humanity.

Yet, this does not remove the freedom of choice from man: "Even as a slave, man retains a certain freedom in that he freely does the bidding of sin."[7] Man still makes free choices, but he freely chooses sin. Put another way, the human will that was corrupted in the fall, is free. This freedom, however, is limited to its sinful nature, which is oriented towards disobedience. Augustine defines free will as simply doing what one wants to do,

> "Augustine can hold that fallen man is free to sin but not free not to sin, yet still possesses free will, because as a sinner Adam wants to sin. The will is both free and unfree. Hence, Augustine can speak of the "captive free will."[8]

Augustine taught that man is hopelessly lost and incapable of doing anything to save himself. Therefore, grace, which is external to us, must come first. The will must be repaired and changed by grace so that man can obediently respond to God's call. Augustine believed this grace that comes before, called prevenient or preceding grace, repairs the will and allows men to accept the gospel call. This is typically called monergism - mono (one) work - meaning that regeneration or conversion wholly depends upon God's grace without man's cooperation. Stated another way, monergism historically means that the Holy Spirit is the only agent in regeneration and that man does not cooperate in conversion. This is opposed to synergism, wherein man cooperates with God in order to be converted.

According to Augustine, all men are born as children of wrath because of Adam, and God is under no compulsion to save anyone. In his mercy, God gives prevenient grace to some, but not all. Augustine believed the reason for this is unknown - the secret judgments of God. At this point, God elects (chooses) some to be saved. This is typically called Particular Predestination. Yet Augustine held that some of the elect could fall away from the faith in a type of temporal election, lacking the gift of perseverance. The question raised at this point is: does God also elect the unregenerate (or unbelievers), predestining them to hell? Augustine's answer to this question is debated. Peterson argues "no," saying that for Augustine, God only elects the regenerate and *passes by* the unregenerate, leaving them in their current state justly.[9] Others would argue that he held to "double predestination," where *God actively elects both the regenerate to salvation and the unregenerate to hell.*

The discussion can get muddied on "double predestination," as Calvinists will point out that God's choosing who will be saved logically predestines those he passes over. In other words, predestination is always double, but with an active aspect (to salvation) and a passive aspect (to damnation). Some who adopt this active and passive schema will reject the 'double predestination' label and instead say they hold to 'single predestination.' What is often thought of as 'double predestination' is the idea that God elects both groups actively. Sometimes this is referred to as equal ultimacy, where the election to salvation and damnation is done in parallel and in an identical fashion rather than in an active/passive model. However, we can press on with the question about Augustine's position on this issue unattended.

Detour on Monergism and Synergism

While the terms monergism and synergism arise in many debates, I have become convinced that monergism and synergism are generally unhelpful terms to utilize regarding soteriology. This is because the words are not unanimously understood the same way and also because of how they are used in polemics.

For example, it is often asserted that synergism is a type of cooperation between two equals: those two equals being man and God. This would necessitate that synergism falls into Pelagianism or semi-Pelagianism. However, most openly synergistic systems deny this. Instead, they say that the synergism (or cooperation) is merely man's free response to God's grace. It is essentially an active acceptance of God's grace rather than rejecting it. On the other hand, if synergism is taken to mean something like a man can will enough and then becomes regenerated, this is incorrect and indeed falls into semi-Pelagianism, as I will explain below.

The use of these terms becomes even more puzzling if we compare two systems that speak similarly. We will be using Lutheranism and Classical Arminianism as our examples. Lutheranism avoids synergism by stating that man *passively receives God's grace* (contrary to actively accepting God's grace) but can actively reject God's grace. Therefore, they would claim to be monergistic. To Lutherans, because man passively receives God's grace, he does nothing to cooperate with grace for conversion.[10] The problem is that Classical Arminianism makes similar claims and is typically considered synergistic. Looking briefly, and perhaps a bit prematurely, at Classical Arminianism, Matthew Pinson in 40 Questions about Arminianism states,

> "One main concern Calvinists have with Arminianism is that it constitutes synergism, which means working together. Thus, they say, rather than regeneration being monergistic, the work of God alone, Arminian theology makes it synergistic. Somehow, they say, Arminians believe that people are working together or cooperating with God to bring about their salvation. Many Arminians, while they would disagree with the above characterization, still use the term synergism. But Reformed Arminians such as Thomas Helwys, Thomas Grantham, and Arminius himself, would not have wanted to be called synergists."[11]

Quoting Carl Bangs, Pinson states that "although Arminius speaks of cooperation, it is not co-earning as has been pointed out. The cooperation is a result of renewal, not a means towards it."[12] Pinson continues to point out that if we say synergism cannot be attributed to Melanchthon's passive reception of merit, then Arminianism cannot be considered synergistic either as they find agreement.[13] He states,

> "Arminians who avoid the label are much like Lutheran theologians. Despite the fact that many modern scholars neatly divide Lutherans into monergistic and synergistic camps, no good Lutheran ever wanted to be known as a synergist."[14]

Historical Points of Interest

And,

> "early modern Lutherans and their descendants strongly demurred from the label "synergist" that their opponents placed on them. They believed that divine grace could be resisted even after conversion, that one could fall from grace. Yet they strenuously contended that they were not synergists."[15]

While there is much more to this topic, the point is that we won't be utilizing these terms much beyond this brief explanation because they ultimately prove unhelpful. What needs to be understood is that semi-Pelagianism *is* synergistic, but *not all synergistic systems are semi-Pelagian*. With that, we move on to asking what is semi-Pelagianism? Answering this question is crucial to navigating modern discussions on Calvinism, Arminianism, and everything in between.

Semi-Pelagianism

The current scholarship regarding semi-Pelagianism is trickier than that surrounding Pelagianism. Pelagianism is easier to navigate because of its explicit condemnation at an ecumenical council, regardless of whether or not Pelagius himself held to the doctrines condemned. Just as one could argue that Nestorius was not actually Nestorian, we would still argue (and hopefully agree) that the doctrine he was charged with was condemned and is indeed heresy.

As one can guess, scholarship has argued that, like with Pelagius, those charged with semi-Pelagianism were not actually semi-Pelagian. Further aggravating our modern discussion is that what we typically find being condemned as "semi-Pelagianism" does not often reflect what semi-Pelagianism was historically understood to be. This makes things even more complex as the Reformed tradition has often equated resistible grace with synergism and has equated synergism with semi-Pelagianism. This means that for many, semi-Pelagianism is resistible grace (freedom to reject God's grace) or synergism. Yet, as I've pointed out, semi-Pelagianism is synergistic, but not all synergistic systems are semi-Pelagian.

We will proceed with the traditional narrative around semi-Pelagianism, recognizing that those behind the term semi-Pelagianism may have been misunderstood or misrepresented. It is also worth pointing out that the term "semi-Pelagian" itself did not exist until Theodore Beza, or the Lutherans, in the 16th century.[16] Still, the word came to be understood as the designation for those condemned at the Council of Orange in the 5th century.

The semi-Pelagians sought a middle ground between Pelagius and Augustine. They acknowledged the reality of original sin and the necessity of baptism and grace for salvation, but they differed from Augustine's position regarding the distribution of grace and the beginning of salvation (i.e., conversion). Instead, the semi-Pelagians taught that Christ died for all humanity, all people were called to salvation, and God created humanity with free will and an innate inclination to do good. This included the ability to discern between good and evil, to have piety toward God, and the ability to seek God.

Augustine believed these gifts of the freedom of the will and inclination towards spiritual good had been lost in original sin. Everything that pertains to eternal life comes from grace instead of a person's nature. On the contrary, the semi-Pelagians argued that every human being has a principle of good, a gift of nature, an incipient faith, and the ability to turn to God with prayer. The semi-Pelagians taught that man can move in his will and meet grace for salvation. They were synergistic, holding to a cooperation for conversion, but they also had a modified anthropology (the doctrine of man). This modified anthropology said that man could move in his will to God's grace apart from enabling grace. They argued that this ability is still a gift, but it is a gift of creation - natural to man - and this gift allows a person to meet the gift of Christ.

To summarize, the semi-Pelagians taught that men, by the gift of creation, were able to exercise goodwill toward

God apart from any grace. Orton Wiley defines it simply as,

> "It held that there was sufficient power remaining in the depraved will to initiate or set in motion the beginnings of salvation but not enough to bring it to completion. This must be done by divine grace."[17]

Put another way,

> "The Semi-Pelagians insisted that human beings cannot be saved apart from the supernatural assisting grace of God. But the fallen human will is not held in bondage to sin; it is not completely disabled by sinful corruption. Human beings can, unaided by grace, take the first step towards salvation."[18]

And,

> "In Semi-Pelagian synergism, human beings are the initiators of faith. Grace is responsive to our search for God and the good. God helps those who help themselves."[19]

A key event in the discussions was a local synod or council in Orange, France, held in AD 529. This event was prompted by a debate between the semi-Pelagians and Augustine on his conception of predestination. This local council upheld Augustine's position on the fall of Adam, its effects on humanity, and the necessity of God's grace in salvation. However, this council did not uphold Augustine's exact position on predestination or the concept of irresistible grace. Instead, as the Calvinist Herman Bavinck summarizes in his Reformed Dogmatics, "The Synod of Orange...accepted prevenient grace but did not decisively adopt irresistible grace and particular predestination."[20]

Again, Prevenient grace is a grace that "comes before" and frees man from the bondage of sin, allowing man to respond to the gospel. Irresistible grace will be defined later, but it is sufficient for now to say that the council of Orange allowed for synergistic systems that begin with grace. Arminian Roger Olson states,

> "Semi-Pelagianism was condemned by the Second Council of Orange in AD 529 because it affirmed human ability to exercise a good will toward God apart from special assistance of divine grace; it places the initiative in salvation on the human side, but scripture places it on the divine side."[21]

The documents of the council of Orange stressed the corruption of human nature, including that man's will is enslaved to sin. Therefore, the whole man has been corrupted and cannot move towards God without a prevenient grace. This prevenient grace is necessary and works in a man to free their will to allow or enable man to respond to God's gift of salvation. The canons of the council stress that no sinner can come to God by his own will. Instead, God must act first. This grace is necessary for a repaired will, conversion, and good works (*See Appendix B*). Peterson and Williams are helpful again,

"The synod softened the Augustinian teaching into a gracious synergism. First, as stated above, the synod did not endorse predestination. The canons explicitly reject predestination to damnation, but they are completely silent concerning predestination to redemption. Second, while the synod insisted that the initiation of faith begins with the work of grace, it suggested that human agency cooperates with the divine in order to produce redemption. This synergism is subtly but crucially different from that of the Semi-Pelagians. While both see redemption as the product of both divine grace and human effort, the semi-Pelagians depict redemption as beginning with human agency. The Semi-Augustinian synergism of Orange reversed the sequence. Hence, a person's contribution to salvation is faithful response to the grace of God. Grace is prevenient here in that it precedes human response."[22]

This discussion is relevant for a couple of reasons. First, the history of semi-Pelagianism acts as a caution to any new system that posits a position of corruption or depravity of human beings that does not include a notion of the total inability of the natural man to respond to grace without some prevenient grace. This is why Classical or Reformed Arminians and others in Wesleyan traditions quickly point out that many self-proclaimed Arminians, or even those labeled Arminians by others, often fall into semi-Pelagianism, if not full-blown Pelagianism.[23]

We will go more in-depth on the Classical Arminian position later. Still, to summarize, the semi-Pelagians thought that salvation began with the inherent freedom of the will, unaided by grace, seeking God and God responding to that seeking. The Remonstrance, or Arminians, held that human will was so corrupted by sin that a person could not seek grace without the enablement of grace. In contrast to the semi-Pelagians, Arminians taught that grace must go before a person's response to the gospel. Thus, it has been said that Arminians could be labeled as semi-Augustinians.[24]

The second reason this is important concerns Reformed polemics against Arminianism, which equates semi-Pelagianism with a denial of irresistible grace. Such a mistake can be found in many admirable Reformed teachers, such as the late R.C. Sproul. Overall, the Reformed tradition has taken the roots of Arminianism and built a strawman to the extent that Robert Godfrey, in his exposition on the Dutch synod against Arminianism, and the Canons of Dort states,

> "As the Reformation was a revival of a biblical Augustinianism, so the Synod of Dort stands in the great Christian heritage that rejects Pelagianism and Semi-Pelagianism."[25]

Godfrey went on to write about Arminianism because it holds that man can reject saving grace (I.e., does not hold to irresistible grace), "it sounds like a theology that tries to be as Augustinian as possible but in the end remains semi-Pelagian."[26] Godfrey's logic here begs the question of whether Lutherans have a theology that tries to be as Augustinian as possible but fails to reach it since

Lutheranism rejects irresistible grace as the Arminians did. Nonetheless, in Calvinist literature, we often find the equation between Arminianism and semi-Pelagianism with little distinction between Classical Arminianism and those who defected from it. It would be like erroneously calling Calvinists Hyper-Calvinists or even Fatalists. Ultimately, it needs to be stated that Arminianism, in its original articulation, minimally, was not semi-Pelagian. Further, a denial of irresistible grace is not inherently semi-Pelagian.

Reformation Era History

During the periods leading up to the Reformation, there were semi-Pelagian schools of thought, primarily and famously found in the scholastic theologian Gabriel Biel. Gabriel Biel and William of Ockham taught what is known as the via moderna. To summarize, the position taught that if a sinner did his best according to his own natural powers, God would give him grace - essentially, it was neo-Pelagianism. Gabriel Biel elicited Luther's discussions on justification and the bondage of the will with the help of Luther's associate Philip Melanchthon.[27]

Luther in Brief

An important discussion is found in 1524, when the scholar Erasmus, famous for his Greek text of the New Testament, wrote "The Freedom of the Will." Most seem to take the position that Erasmus adopted a semi-Pelagian position in this work, while some argue that Erasmus upheld the council of Orange. For the sake of ease, I'll be taking the former and predominant position. Erasmus addressed Luther's Augustinian theology of sin and grace and argued that salvation was a shared work of human free will and divine grace.

Erasmus sought to say that the human will was ineffective in doing good but had power enough to meet grace.[28] He argued that grace was essential, but man could meet or reject it at any point. It was in 1525 that Luther responded in his work "The Bondage of the Will," wherein Luther restated Augustinian theology while "sometimes going well beyond Augustine."[29]

> "For instance, when Luther said that God's sovereignty in itself excluded human free will, he went beyond Augustine. All Augustine ever said was that the fall of Adam had excluded free will in spiritual matters. Luther's view would mean that not even before he sinned could Adam have had free will, since God's sovereignty operated before as well as after the fall."[30]

These issues led to every Christian party involved in the Reformation era re-affirming anti-semi-Pelagian stances, even in the Catholic Counter-Reformation. While it is asserted that Catholicism did this inconsistently, they formally uphold that they rejected semi-Pelagianism at the Council of Trent. According to Catholics, this can be seen in chapter 5, session 6, canon 3 of Trent, which states,

> "If anyone says that without the predisposing inspiration of the Holy Ghost and without his help, man can believe, hope, love, or be repentant as he ought, so that the grace of justification may be bestowed upon him, let him be anathema."

Trent seems to be semi-Pelagian only if one incorrectly claims that semi-Pelagianism includes the will's response post-prevenient grace, which it does not. That said, I'll leave the discussion on Catholicism to those more inclined to it. Before closing out our historical discussion, we will briefly discuss the Calvinists and Arminians.

Beza and Arminius

Contrary to popular belief, it is after John Calvin's life that we find more formal developments within Calvinism. This is due to his successor and son-in-law, Theodore Beza. Beza would head the Academy in Geneva until he passed in 1605. As Peterson and Williams summarize, "Most of the participants in the Arminian controversy - including Jacob Arminius - would be trained at Geneva under his [Bezas] tutelage."[31] They continue,

> "Where the first generation of reformers equated theology with biblical exposition, the successors of Luther and Calvin moved toward the development of theological systems. They sought to organize, fill out and defend the thought of the reformers. And, as was the case more often than not among the systematizers, Beza employed medieval scholasticism...The revival of scholasticism introduced into Reformed theology a greater emphasis upon philosophical and metaphysical concerns than Calvin entertained."[32]

It is at this point that most early discussions on what is called supralapsarianism and infralapsarianism were formed. These terms are two of three views within early Calvinism, with Beza holding to the former. These views deal with the logical (opposed to temporal or necessarily temporal) order of God's divine decrees. Supralapsarianism placed God's decrees in the following order:

1. God elects some to salvation and reprobation of others to damnation.
2. God creates the universe.
3. God decrees the fall into sin (Plans the fall).
4. God decrees to provide a savior for the elect via Christ.

In this view, God's election and reprobation come before creation. Thus, creation is for the sake of salvation, and the fall serves God's elective purposes. This view is sometimes called high Calvinism. Another view reflected in the Reformed confessions was infralapsarianism (classic or mainline Calvinism). This view held that God's elective decree is logically after man's fall. Infralapsarianism placed God's decrees in the following order:

1. God's decree to create the world.
2. The decree to allow man to fall into sin through his own self-determination (Permits the fall).
3. God's decree to elect some to salvation and leave others (the non-elect) to their just fate and condemnation.
4. God decrees to provide a savior for the elect via Christ.

This view disagreed with supralapsarianism in that man is essentially created within the supralapsarian scheme for the sake of election and reprobation. Put another way; God created in order to save and condemn and actively predestines men to hell as he causes the fall. Contrary to this, infralapsarianism makes election and passive reprobation occur in order to deal with men who have fallen in Adam. While we will not expand on these two concepts in this book, they are helpful terms to be aware of. Furthermore, we must not believe that the Arminians excluded themselves from discussing the logical order of God's decrees.

Logical Order of God's Decrees Proposed

	Supralapsarianism (High Calvinism)	Infralapsarianism (Mainline, or Classical, Calvinism)	Amyraldism (Low/four point Calvinism)	Arminianism
1	God elects some to salvation and reprobation of others to damnation	God's decree to create the world	God's decree to create the world	God's decree to create the world
2	God creates the universe	The decree to allow man to fall into sin through his own self-determination (Permits the fall)	The decree to allow man to fall into sin through his own self-determination (Permits the fall)	The decree to allow man to fall into sin through his own self-determination (Permits the fall)
3	God decrees the fall into sin (Plans the fall)	God's decree to elect some to salvation and leave others (the non-elect) to their just fate and condemnation	God decrees to provide a savior sufficient for all via Christ	God decrees to provide a savior sufficient for all via Christ
4	God decrees to provide a savior for the elect via Christ	God decrees to provide a savior for the elect via Christ	God's decree to elect some to salvation and leave others (the non-elect) to their just fate and condemnation	Call all to salvation, [5] elect those who have repented and believed

During this period, Jacob Arminius, a student of Beza, came to disagree with various points of theology present in his day. Despite such disagreements, Arminius still confessed the Belgic Confession and Heidelberg Catechism - the two forms of unity of Reformed Churches - before it became the three forms of unity (that came to include the Canons of Dort).

At this point, the details of the nature and character of Arminius, the Remonstrance (followers of Arminius), and the history around the debates become convoluted. I have personally found the more critical presentation of the Remonstrance to be found wanting. For a treatment of the discussion from a balanced perspective by Calvinists, one can look to Robert Peterson and Michael Williams, "Why I am not an Arminian," and for the Arminian side, one can consult Matthew Pinson's "40 Questions about Arminianism." For a critical presentation of the Remonstrance, one can read Robert Godfrey's "Saving the Reformation," specifically his appendices dealing with scholarship surrounding Arminius. Relying on Peterson and Williams primarily, we find,

> "In 1587 Arminius took a pastorate in the Reformed church. While he was an effective and beloved pastor, throughout the 1590s his preaching and teaching incurred the increasing suspicion of the strict Calvinists in and around Amsterdam who judged him as placing too much emphasis on human freedom in the process of belief and repentance. Between 1591 and 1596 Arminius presented his developing views on human free will and predestination in a series of sermons on Romans 7 and 9...Although his preaching earned him the displeasure of a number of other pastors, Arminius remained on good terms with his

own congregation throughout his Amsterdam pastorate."[33]

Arminius taught theology at the University of Leiden in 1603, wherein controversy arose due to tensions with Gomarus, a student of Beza and a strict supralapsarian who would go on to accuse Arminius of theological error. This tension rippled through the Reformed Churches leading to many pastors and laypeople picking sides. Gomarus accused Arminius of deviating from the confessional standards of the Reformed Church (the Belgic Confession and Heidelberg Catechism). Arminius defended himself against the charge in his "Declaration of Sentiments," penned in 1608.

Arminius argued that the confessions were not specific enough for the accusations levied at him, and within this declaration, he argued against supralapsarianism and laid out his objections to it. Arminius did not only reject supralapsarianism, however, but also infralapsarianism and unconditional election as a whole. Unconditional election will be more fully defined and discussed as we work through TULIP, but it taught that God elected some to salvation simply out of his will and *without* consideration of what a man may do in his life.

Arminius presented conditional election, which is the belief that man's election by God is based on God's knowledge of that man's positive response to God's grace and having faith. According to Arminius, neither election nor reprobation is *causal* but is instead based on contingent causes (human choices), so this election is conditional. Yet, Arminius believed God predestines all who will believe in

Christ to be saved and all who reject the gospel to be damned. These are general classes for Arminius - one is either in Christ or outside of Christ. The discussion doesn't end here but must be fleshed out in a later chapter. Arminius insisted that he was not a Pelagian, affirming that salvation's initiation is by God's grace alone and through faith alone. Arminius thought the will is freed via prevenient grace, and the elect are saved through faith, which is a gift of God. Like the Lutherans, Arminius stated that the will of the sinner may resist the enabling that God gives to the sinner. Grace is not causal but rather persuasive in nature, and God cannot coerce belief. For Arminius, the gospel call does not say "you will," but rather "you should."[34] Peterson and Williams state,

> "The real center of the Remonstrance and the lynchpin of the Arminian approach to salvation is found in the phrase, 'this prevenient or assisting, awakening, consequent and cooperating grace.' This phrase places the Arminian articles firmly in the synergistic tradition of the semi-Augustinians. Salvation is a matter of both God and the sinner doing their part. God begins by giving each sinner sufficient repairing grace that he or she is enabled to freely accept or reject the gospel. Human beings, who were formerly unable to contribute the slightest to their own redemption, who were depraved by and enslaved to sin, are sufficiently restored by God's gift of prevenient grace so that they are able to choose for or against the work of Christ."[35]

Historical Points of Interest

After some controversy, those who agreed with Arminius wanted to call a national synod to discuss their disagreements. Unfortunately, Arminius died from illness before it could happen, and in 1610, those who found agreement with Arminius would issue a document to the States General known as a Remonstrance. This is where they would get their name from. The Remonstrance Articles of 1610 contained the five points of Arminianism (*see Appendix C*). They are as follows:

1. Conditional Election
2. Universal Atonement
3. Total Depravity and Prevenient Grace
4. Resistible Grace
5. Conditional Perseverance.

The States General eventually called a synod, now known as the Synod of Dort. This was a national Synod of Reformed churches in Dordrecht, Netherlands. While this Synod was Dutch, it had an international reach with 26 delegates from eight other countries. The Synod of Dort treated the Remonstrance as defendants, charged them with heresy, and required them to appear before the Synod and respond to the charges. The Remonstrance rejected this discussion method and withdrew from the proceedings. The Canons of Dort (*see Appendix D*) were formed at this synod, which are those responses to the Remonstrance's Articles of 1610. The Synod of Dort responded to each of the five points of Arminianism. The Arminians were considered guilty of heresy, with over 200

Arminian pastors being deposed from their posts in congregations and ex-communicated.

Five Points of Arminianism & Calvinism

	Five Points of Arminianism from the Remonstrance Articles of 1610	Summary of the Canons of Dort, 1619, Calvinism	TULIP (Calvinism)
1	Conditional Election	Unconditional Election	T - Total Depravity
2	Universal Atonement	Limited Atonement	U - Unconditional Election
3	Total Depravity and Prevenient Grace	Total Depravity	L - Limited Atonement
4	Resistible Grace	Irresistible Grace	I - Irresistible Grace
5	Conditional Perserverance	Perseverance of the Saints	P - Perseverance of the Saints

It is from the Canons of Dort where TULIP comes from, but the documents of Dort do not follow the order of TULIP, nor are the Canons limited to the often oversimplified presentation of TULIP. The Canons address positive beliefs, rejections of errors, and pastoral concerns. Furthermore, the Canons of Dort remain one of the official standards of the Reformed Tradition, with its doctrines being reflected in Calvinistic confessions such as the Westminster Standards and the London Baptist Confession of Faith.

Nonetheless, TULIP's most well-known order is as follows: Total Depravity, Unconditional Election, Limited Atonement, Irresistible Grace, and Perseverance of the Saints. While many have erroneously focused solely on critiquing Calvin (some of his "adherence" to TULIP is debated!) to address Calvinism, one who wishes to deal with Calvinism accurately must interact with the Canons of Dort. We will save further examinations for the subsequent chapters. This brief history, however, should help orient some of those discussions.

Chapter 2
Total Depravity

Our first theological consideration is the doctrine of total depravity. This chapter will discuss original sin (and guilt) along with the depth of depravity, the will's relationship to sin, and human responsibility. We will begin by defining original sin, then comparing Calvinism and Arminianism's views on original sin and guilt. While separating original sin from guilt may seem bizarre for some readers, it is a distinction that will aid in future discussions while highlighting a point of agreement between most Arminians and Calvinists. Furthermore, one will notice that many of the present discussions are much easier to navigate than other topics in this volume because of the general consensus across traditions.

Original Sin Introduced

Original sin is the doctrine that upholds that man is inherently sinful from birth because of the fall of Adam in the garden of Eden. The doctrine teaches that Adam's sin corrupts all people. Individuals are born with a corrupt nature, inclined to sin and death, without hope for salvation apart from God's grace. This belief is held across all theological traditions, with subtle differences in *how* original sin is transmitted and whether or not it includes the concept of original guilt. Original guilt is the idea that all people are born with the guilt of Adam's sin. For example, within Eastern Orthodoxy is found the doctrine of Ancestral Sin. In essence, this is another way of saying original sin though it does not include original guilt. In the Orthodox tradition, man is still understood as having a sinful inclination - a spiritual disease. This is how the East can hold to the pronouncement against Pelagius at the council of Ephesus in AD 431 - by upholding corruption but not guilt.

We'll summarize the positions below on the dynamic between original sin and guilt. First, however, we must point out that God created mankind to be upright, and sin is a corruption of God's good creation. In the garden of Eden, Adam and Eve chose to disobey God and bring about what is referred to as the fall in Genesis 3. Since then, humans have lived in a patterned inclination of corruption and sin. Sin is wrongdoing, rebellion, unrighteousness, and transgression against God's design and commands. For clarity, sin can therefore be summarized

Total Depravity

as failing to conform to God's design and standards or explicitly opposing them.

The Bible points out that every person sins (Psalm 53:1-3; Jeremiah 17:9; Romans 3:10-23). Everyone, except the incarnate Son of God, experiences spiritual and moral corruption. Thus, each human being has the impending reality of death and eternal punishment apart from God's saving grace. Ephesians 2:3 points out that "we were children of wrath just like the others" before our salvation. In that same chapter, human beings are described as dead in trespasses and sins, following the sinful course of the world and the devil. Genesis 8:21 states, "The imagination of man's heart is evil from his youth," and Psalm 58:13 continues, "The wicked are estranged from the womb; they go astray as soon as they are born speaking lies."

Christendom has agreed that sin is universal because it affects the whole of creation. Every person is impacted by sin. Even Jesus, who was without sin, was crucified by sinful people. The impact of sin is universal, and aside from Christ, "all have sinned and fall short of the glory of God" (Romans 3:23). Sin has been the human condition since the fall of Adam and Eve. This condition's cure is found in the person and work of Jesus upon the cross and his resurrection. Sin is the disease, and Christ is the cure. This all points to the reality that without God's grace, we are without hope - we are helpless to save ourselves.

As mentioned, we can properly distinguish some differences in the concept of original sin by considering the relationship between the idea of inherited guilt and inherited consequence. The former says that people inherit not only the inclination to sin and mortality from

Adam but also Adam's guilt. The latter disagrees with Adam's guilt being included in the conception of original sin. Here is a helpful summary of those dynamics and differing views, with some respective adherents compiled by Adam Harwood in Calvinism: A Biblical and Theological Critique:

> "1. Symbolic and existential interpretations—deny the existence or importance of Adam and Eve (F. R. Tennant, Paul Tillich)
>
> 2. Corruption-only doctrines—corruption without corresponding guilt due to Adam's sin (Christian theology before Augustine, the Orthodox Church, Ulrich Zwingli, Richard Swinburne, Stanley Grenz)
>
> 3. Corruption and guilt: federalism—all people are guilty of Adam's sin because he represented humanity in the garden (Francis Turretin)
>
> 4. Corruption and guilt: realism—all people are guilty of Adam's sin because they were present with him in the garden (Augustine, Jonathan Edwards)
>
> 5. Corruption and guilt: mediate views—all people are guilty due to the corruption from original sin, not for the sins of Adam and Eve (Anselm, John Calvin, Henri Blocher)
>
> 6. Conditional imputation of guilt—all people

Total Depravity

ratify the guilt of Adam when they knowingly commit their first act of sin (Millard Erickson)."[1]

As we have stated, since all traditions agree on the reality of corruption via the fall of Adam in the garden, the discussion on original sin is easiest to navigate without considering original guilt. However, original guilt will briefly be highlighted to compare and contrast Calvinism and Arminianism.

Original Guilt

Due to its complex nature, much time could be spent on the issue of original guilt. This becomes especially true in light of historical theology, as inherited guilt appears to be unknown before Augustine. Church Historian Gerald Bray states, "It is virtually an axiom of historical theology that the doctrine of original sin, as we recognize it today, cannot be traced back beyond Augustine."[2] Further, Bray points out that Christians in the East, mostly unconcerned with the Pelagian controversies, assumed mortality was the result of Adam's sin without indication of imputed guilt, but rather the corruption of our nature, most clearly articulated by Cyril of Alexandria.[3] In the Western tradition, however, original sin with guilt was predominant. Imputation refers to the transfer of benefit or harm from one individual to another,[4] or "setting to someone's account or reckoning something to another person."[5] The Holman Illustrated Bible Dictionary puts forward this example,

> "God reckoned righteousness to believing Abraham (Gen. 15:6). This means that God credited to Abraham that which he did not have in himself (Rom. 4:3-5). This does not mean that God accepted Abraham's faith instead of righteousness as an accomplishment meriting justification. Rather, it means that God accepted Abraham because he trusted in God rather than trusting in something that he could do."[6]

Total Depravity

When addressing the imputation of Adam's guilt, we are talking about crediting the guilt of his sin to his descendants. In the same manner, if we speak about the imputation of Christ's righteousness, we are talking about crediting the righteousness of Christ to those in Christ. A key text in the discussion around original guilt is Romans 5:12-19. Beginning with 12-14, it is as follows:

> "Therefore, just as sin came into the world through one man, and death through sin, and so death spread to all men because all sinned— for sin indeed was in the world before the law was given, but sin is not counted where there is no law. Yet death reigned from Adam to Moses, even over those whose sinning was not like the transgression of Adam, who was a type of the one who was to come." (Romans 5:12–14)

There is little debate when it comes to whether or not it was through Adam that sin entered the world. It is also generally agreed upon that death came through sin. Death is presented as the consequence of sin, which has come into the world, "spread to all men." Christians concur that sin is universal, and all die because of sin.

The dispute concerns the phrase, "So death spread to all men *because all sinned*" (my emphasis). The debate on this line is most often because of how Augustine translated the Greek phrase. Augustine's reading would read, "Death spread to all men in whom (Adam) all sinned" or, "all men sinned in Adam." This would mean that all of Adam's subsequent children sinned with Adam and thus are born with original guilt. The issue is that the phrase here is best translated using the word "because."[7] Douglas Moo states that the rendering and interpretation of Augustine are likely incorrect as the two words in Greek are probably functioning as a conjunction meaning something like "from which it follows," "with the result that," etc."[8] The Greek phrase can also be found in texts like 2 Corinthians 5:4 and Philippians 3:2. Moo states, "Paul's concern in this verse…is not with original sin, but with original death…but we cannot stop here"[9] because verses 15-19 are just as crucial for the subject. They state,

> "But the free gift is not like the trespass. For if many died through one man's trespass, much more have the grace of God and the free gift by the grace of that one man Jesus Christ abounded for many. And the free gift is not like the result of that one man's sin. For the judgment following one trespass brought condemnation, but the free gift following many trespasses brought justification. For if, because of one man's trespass, death reigned through that one man, much more will those who receive the abundance of grace and the free gift of righteousness reign in life through the one man Jesus Christ.
>
> Therefore, as one trespass led to condemnation for all men, so one act of righteousness leads to justification and life for all men. For as by the one man's disobedience the many were made sinners, so by the one man's obedience the many will be made righteous." (Romans 5:15–19)

Total Depravity

The questions that arise are: *How* does the *one trespass* lead to the condemnation *of all men*? Is Adam's sin the *cause* of our condemnation or the *means* of our condemnation? (condemnation implying our guilt).[10] With these questions in mind, we can begin to compare our theological systems of Calvinism and Classical Arminianism.

Calvinism on Original Guilt

Along with much of the Western tradition, Calvinists and Reformed Theology generally holds that all men are born with both sin and guilt, "for there cannot be sin without guilt any more than fire without smoke, heat, or light."[11] Douglas Moo, who rejects the "In Adam" translation of Romans 5:12, goes on to point out regarding Romans 5:15-19,

> "if we read v. 12 in light of 18-19, because of the comparative clauses repeat the substance of v. 12…'all sinned' must be given some kind of corporate meaning: sinning not as voluntary acts of sin in one's own person, but sinning in and with Adam. This is not to adopt the translation in Adam reject above. The point is rather that the sin here attributed to the 'all' is the be understood…as a sin that in some manner is identical to the sin committed by Adam. Paul can therefore say both that 'all die because all sin' and 'all die because Adam sinned' with no hint of conflict because the sin of Adam is the sin of all. All people, therefore, stand condemned 'in Adam,' guilty by reason of the sin all committed in him. This interpretation is defended by a great number of exegetes and theologians. It maintains the close connection between Adam's sin and the condemnation of all that is required by vv. 15-19, a connection suggested also by 1 Corinthians 15:22 - "In Adam all die." And a sin committed before individual consciousness also explains how Paul could consider all people as 'by nature children of wrath' (Eph. 2:3)."[12]

Total Depravity

Michael Patton, from Credo House, succinctly and helpfully outlines the comparison between Adam and Christ.

"Whatever one does with Christ's righteousness, one must do with Adam's sin...Let us take a look at this comparison. Through Adams Sin Judgment (16) Condemnation (16) Death Reigned (17) One Transgression = Condemnation of all (18) Adam's disobedience = many were made sinners (19) Through Christ's Righteousness Free gift (16) Justification (16) Life Reigned (17) One Act of Righteousness = Justification of all (18) Christ's obedience = many were made righteous (19)."

He states,

"The comparison is unmistakable. Again, whatever we do to inherit the free gift is the same thing we did to inherit judgment (v. 16). This is the force of the "just as" (hosper) in v. 12. Whatever we do to receive justification is the same thing we did to receive condemnation (v. 16). The effects of the "one act of righteousness" are brought about by the same means as the "condemnation of all men" (v. 18). The way in which believers are made righteous is analogous to the way all mankind was made sinners (v. 19). In order to answer the question as to how it is that "all sinned" and all were condemned in Adam, we must answer the question as to how Christ's righteousness is applied to us to the end that we are justified by that righteousness.

If we were to adopt the view as held by Pelagius, that Adam's sin has no effect upon us whatsoever and that only his example has given us trouble, this means that Christ's righteousness has no effect upon us either. He simply came to set the example. But this is not what the text teaches. It states that the many were made sinners and that the many were made righteous. The effect of these two men's acts goes far beyond that of an example.

Paul is attempting to explain our relationship to Christ's righteousness by comparing it to the imputation of Adam's sin to us. This relationship, in my opinion, is best seen in the federal headship view of imputation. As Doug Moo puts it, "Throughout this whole passage what Adam did and what Christ did are steadily held over against each other. Now salvation in Christ does not mean that we merit salvation by living good lives; rather, what Christ has done is significant. Just so, death in Adam does not mean that we are being punished for our own evil deeds; it is what Adam has done that is significant."[13]

The Canons of Dort, in article 1, under the first point of doctrine, summarizes, "As all men have sinned in Adam, lie under the curse, and are deserving of eternal death." The Westminster Confession of Faith states, "They (Adam and Eve) being the root of all mankind, the guilt of this sin was imputed; and the same death in sin, and corrupted natured, conveyed to all their posterity descending from them by ordinary generation." (6.3) Furthermore, this is also present in the particular Baptist's[14] confession of faith (The London Baptist Confession) in chapter 6, section 3, which is close to the Westminster Confession on the subject,

> "the guilt of sin was imputed and corrupted nature conveyed, to all their posterity descending from them by ordinary generation, being conceived in Sin, and by nature children of wrath."

In Calvinism and Reformed theology, Adam's guilt and sin - our judicial or legal guilt - is taken up by Christ on our behalf on the cross and is exchanged for Christ's perfect righteousness by faith.

> "As Romans 4:5 tells us, when we put our faith in Christ, we are counted as righteous. That is, the perfect righteousness earned by Jesus is imputed to us. In turn, our sins are imputed to Jesus who made satisfaction for them by bearing the wrath of God against His people on the cross.
>
> God's law tells us that we can never be good enough to be righteous in His sight. The gospel tells us that Christ is perfectly righteous and that by faith alone His righteousness is credited to us."[15]

Arminianism on Original Guilt

Discussing Arminianism, Matthew Pinson states, "Arminius openly affirmed and defended the Reformed statements on original sin and total depravity in the Belgic Confession of Faith and Heidelberg Catechism."[16] Jacob Arminius, in his Apology against Thirty-One-Defamatory Articles, would go on to state,

> "the whole of this sin ... is not peculiar to our first parents, but is common to the entire race and to all their posterity, who, at the time when this sin was committed, were in their loins, and who have since descended from them by the natural mode of propagation."[17]

And,

> "For in Adam 'all have sinned.' (Romans 5:12). Wherefore, whatever punishment was brought down upon our first parents, has likewise pervaded and yet pursues all their posterity: So that all men 'are by nature the children of wrath', obnoxious to condemnation and to temporal as well as to eternal death; they are also devoid of that original righteousness and holiness. With these evils they would remain oppressed forever, unless they were liberated by Christ Jesus; to whom be glory for ever."[18]

Pinson continues,

Total Depravity

"When asked the question, "Is the guilt of original sin taken away from all and every one by the benefits of Christ?" Arminius said that "deliverance from this guilt" is a benefit of union with Christ and thus "believers only are delivered from it." Furthermore, Arminius said that God "imputed the guilt of the first sin to all Adam's posterity, no less than to Adam himself and Eve, because they also had sinned in Adam."[19]

As with the Calvinist mentioned before, Jacob Arminius stated, "Justification is purely the imputation of righteousness through mercy from the throne of grace in Christ the propitiation made to a sinner, but who is a believer."[20]

Arminian Leroy Forlines spends a couple of pages focused on this point in his book Classical Arminianism. Looking at Romans 5:12-19, Forlines states plainly, "Romans 5:12-19 definitely settles the fact that the sin of Adam is imputed or placed on the account of the whole race."[21] Forlines takes the position of Natural Headship over and against Federal Headship, though we will not focus on that divergence here. Forlines goes on to look at the parallel between the imputation of Adam's sin and the imputation of Christ's death and righteousness. He says,

> "Another view that is frequently referred to as the Arminian view does not teach that the race is charged with the guilt of Adam's sin...While it is true that Some Arminians have advocated this view, it is by no means universally accepted and should not be called the Arminian view. This is especially true since it was not

the view held by Arminius himself. It is somewhat puzzling why people with good scholarly credentials would say that Arminius denied the imputation of Adam's sin to the race."[22]

Some within the camp of Classical Arminianism would say that the atonement of Christ set aside Adam's *guilt* of original sin but not the *corruption* of original sin. All inherit a corrupt human nature, making actual sins and guilt inevitable. It can be said that on the subject of original guilt, Classical Arminians and Calvinists generally find agreement except on the issue of how the sin of Adam is transmitted (Federal vs. Natural headship).

The Corruption of Man

Following our discussion on original guilt, we can begin looking at the corruption of man and the extent of that corruption according to Calvinism and Classical Arminianism. This means looking at depravity and the depth of that depravity. Due to the high level of agreement amongst Calvinists and Arminians on the subject, I will outline what depravity is first and foremost. This will be followed with a key text on the issue, and then we will move on to Calvinist and Arminian sources on the subject to compare. This section will also touch on the human will concerning the fall, but not the discussion of human will in the broader sense. That will be discussed in the next chapter. We will begin with a basic definition of depravity according to the Pocket Dictionary of Theological Terms,

> "*Depravity* refers both to the damaged relationship between God and humans and to the corruption of human nature such that there is within every human an ongoing tendency toward sin. *Total depravity* refers to the extent and comprehensiveness of the effects of sin on all humans such that all are unable to do anything to obtain salvation. Total depravity, therefore, does not mean that humans are thoroughly sinful but rather that they are totally incapable of saving themselves. The term suggests as well that the effects of the Fall extend to every dimension of human existence, so that we dare not trust any ability (such as reason) that we remain capable of exercising in our fallen state."[23]

As we can see, there are several things that depravity is not. Relying on Daniel's work on Calvinism, total depravity is not the universal sinfulness of man but, more specifically, that all parts of men are sinful.[24] Furthermore,

> "Total depravity is also more than extreme cases of sin. We do not say that only gross criminals like Hitler are totally depraved, and the rest of us are not. Some sins are worse than others (John 19:11), and some sinners are worse than others (1 Timothy 3:13). But even the least sinner with the fewest sins is totally depraved. All cups are full, but some cups are larger than others. We are all full of sin."[25]

He continues to point out that total depravity does not eliminate our humanity, nor do we forfeit the image of God, nor does total depravity equal demonic possession.[26] Ultimately total depravity means that the nature of man "has been so thoroughly affected by original sin that every part of his being is under the control of sin."[27] All of man is affected – it is total. Jeremiah 17:9 informs us about the wickedness of the heart, while Jesus tells us that wickedness flows from it (Matthew 15:18-19). Ecclesiastes points out, "Truly the hearts of the sons of men are full of evil; madness is in their hearts while they live" (9:3). This notion of the corruption of the heart is found throughout the scriptures from Genesis onward. The heart must be recognized as the center of a human being: it is the core of who a human being is,[28] and the human heart has been radically affected by the fall.

Not only has sin corrupted man through the heart, but

the mind has also been affected. The Proverbs state, "The thoughts of the wicked are an abomination to the Lord" (15:26). Paul describes those without the light of God's grace as having futility of thinking and darkened understanding (Ephesians 4:17-19). In his fallen state, man cannot comprehend divine truth (1 Corinthians 2:14; Romans 3:11) and are naturally inclined to plot from their disposition of sinful desires (Jeremiah 4:22). This truth can be applied to other aspects of the human condition. Still, the portions necessary for our discussion are these truths concerning the human will and whether or not the will is included in the total depravity of man.

As the will is a faculty of nature, and man's heart has been corrupted, it follows that the will has also been affected. Man has the freedom of will to make choices and movements in life, but when it comes to matters of spiritual importance, man's disposition is to move freely towards sin rather than God. By nature, men choose death rather than life (Deuteronomy 30:19; Job 15:16).

We'll focus on one text that exemplifies this reality, but first, a distinction needs to be made. We see men doing good things daily, but how does this work with the doctrine outlined so far? These good deeds (or natural good) in the world must be distinguished from spiritual good. Man can indeed do good deeds, but he does not do them out of love or for the glory of God, making them still sinful acts (1 Corinthians 10:31). Even when the natural man does good, his standing and motive, detached from God, make his good deeds merely external rather than good in a spiritually meaningful sense. That said, we can move to an essential text on total depravity in Romans chapter 3.

> "What then? Are we Jews any better off? No, not at all. For we have already charged that all, both Jews and Greeks, are under sin, as it is written: "None is righteous, no, not one; no one understands; no one seeks for God. All have turned aside; together they have become worthless; no one does good, not even one." "Their throat is an open grave; they use their tongues to deceive." "The venom of asps is under their lips." "Their mouth is full of curses and bitterness." "Their feet are swift to shed blood; in their paths are ruin and misery, and the way of peace they have not known." "There is no fear of God before their eyes." (Romans 3:9–18)

Let's break this down. "What then? Are we Jews any better off? No, not at all. For we have already charged that all, both Jews and Greeks, are under sin," Paul states that while Jews may have historical privileges as God's people, they are still under sin and will be judged impartially. Paul then puts the universal nature of corruption at the forefront. He produces the most extended quotation of the Old Testament in the New Testament, comprised of at least six passages. Paul allows for no exception; all men are included here. Douglas Moo summarizes well,

> "The problem with people is not just that they commit sins; their problem is that they are enslaved to sin. What is needed, therefore, is a new power to break in and set

people free from sin – a power found in, and only in, the gospel of Jesus Christ."[29]

Paul's emphasis on the lack of righteousness, lack of understanding, lack of seeking, and so forth is put forward in vivid language:

"None is righteous, no, not one; no one understands; no one seeks for God. All have turned aside; together they have become worthless; no one does good, not even one." "Their throat is an open grave; they use their tongues to deceive." "The venom of asps is under their lips." "Their mouth is full of curses and bitterness." "Their feet are swift to shed blood; in their paths are ruin and misery, and the way of peace they have not known." "There is no fear of God before their eyes." (Romans 3:9–18)

Paul stresses that the law can justify no one, as all have fallen short. Instead, righteousness comes through faith. In Paul's explanation of all being condemned, we learn that all men are under sin, and none can be seen as righteous. Man does not seek God. Instead, they turn aside and move away from God's purposes and design. Christians across traditions have understood this passage to express man's corruption and humanity's universal sinfulness across traditions. Apart from God's grace and the gospel's message, man's plight is to be left in a just condemnation, for he is under sin, and his disposition is towards sin.

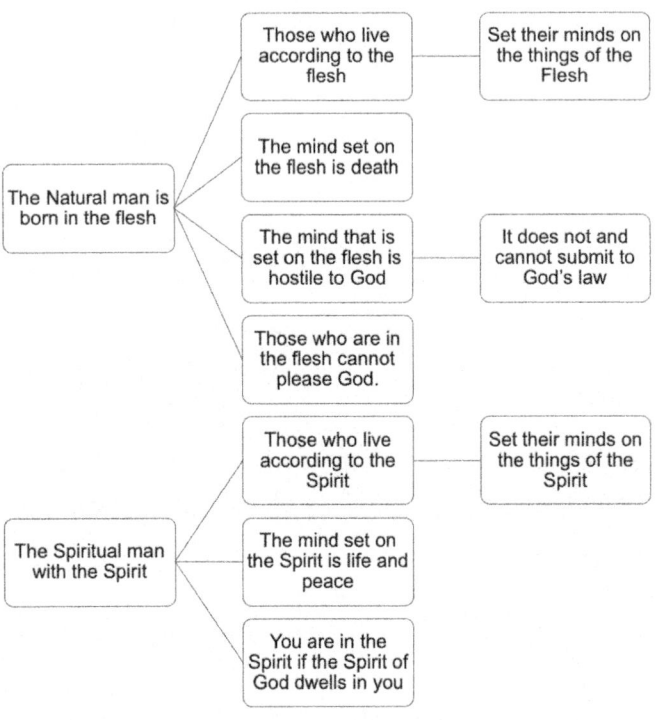

The Paradigm of Romans 8:5-9

Thankfully, Paul's epistle to the Romans didn't end with this plight of man. Instead, he goes on to express the beauty of righteousness through faith in the person and work of Christ. The Christian, with the Holy Spirit, can live according to the Spirit. We will now look at the Classical Arminian's position on Total Depravity.

Arminianism on Total Depravity

We can now place our two theological traditions side by side on the issue of total depravity. In this section, I will have to introduce some essential elements regarding the human will. If the discussion about the human will is confusing after this chapter, take heart as we will spend time on that issue with more detail next. We'll begin our comparison by examining the Arminian position on total depravity. Because of how it is typically presented in the public sphere, we will spend more time here than on the Calvinist side of the discussion.

In 40 Questions about Arminianism, Matthew Pinson wrote a chapter asking, "Are Arminians Semi-Pelagians Who Deny Total Depravity and Total Inability?" Pinson's answer can be summarized with a resounding "no." He states,

> "Pelagians and semi-Pelagians believe that there is, to a greater or lesser degree, some sort of natural free will or ability to respond to the gospel without special grace from the Holy Spirit. It, is however, a gross mischaracterization to say that Arminians believe this. While some who mistakenly claim the name Arminian believe it, traditional Arminians do not."[30]

Pinson is also helpful in summarizing Jacob Arminius on the subject, pointing out that

> "Arminius openly affirmed and defended the Reformed statements on original sin and total depravity in the

Belgic Confession of Faith and the Heidelberg Catechism. He was clear in his affirmation of the Reformed accounts of what would later be called total depravity."[31]

The Belgic Confession in Article 15 details the corruption of all nature as the root that produces every sort of sin in man. Arminius fully held to the concept of original sin and guilt, but he also "believed that people have no ability to seek God or turn to him unless they are moved by his special grace."[32] Arminius taught that man's will is free from necessity, a concept we will discuss later, but that the human will is not free from sin or its dominion.

"The free will of man towards the true good is not only wounded, maimed, infirm, bent, and weakened; but it is also imprisoned, destroyed, and lost: And its powers are not only debilitated and useless unless they be assisted by grace, but it has no powers whatever except such are excited by divine grace."[33]

Arminius argued that the whole person – mind, affections, and will – was affected by the fall. He stated that the human mind "is dark, destitute of the saving knowledge of God, and according to the Apostle, incapable of those things which belong to the Spirit of God."[34] Pinson again summarizes Arminius' position,

"The affections and the heart are perverse, with a hatred and aversion to the true good and to what pleases God, and with a love for evil and the pursuit of it. In their

Total Depravity

deceitful, perverse, uncircumcised, hard, and stony hearts, unregenerate people have set themselves up as enemies of God. The will has no power to perform the true good or keep from committing evil, because the unregenerate are slaves of the devil and under his power. The entire life—mind, heart, and will—is submerged under sin and dead in sin. These views led Moses Stuart to aver that "the most thorough advocate of total depravity will scarcely venture to go farther in regard to man in his unregenerate state, than Arminius goes."[35]

Thus, without grace, man is not able to come to God. Those who followed Arminius - the Remonstrance - followed in this affirmation. The Five Articles of the Remonstrance declared, "That man has not saving grace of himself, nor the energy of his free will, inasmuch as he, in the state of apostasy and sin, can of and by himself neither think, will, nor do anything that is truly good." The Remonstrance Confession of 1621 produced after the Synod of Dort stated, "because Adam was the stock and root of all mankind, therefore, he involved and entangled, not only himself, but also all his posterity in the same death and misery with himself."[36] The General Baptists then followed Arminius, though not without dissenters, which is documented in the Orthodox Creed of 1678. They asserted that original sin,

> "is the fault and corruption of the nature of every man naturally descendeth from Adam by natural generation; by means of which man has not only lost that original

righteousness, that God created him in, but is naturally inclined to all manner of evil...after the fall, man wholly lost all ability, or liberty of will, to any spiritual good, for his eternal salvation, his will being now in bondage under sin and Satan; and therefore not able of his own strength to convert himself, nor prepare himself thereunto, without God's grace."[37]

The Wesleyan Movement followed suit in its Methodist Articles of Religion of 1784, stating that after the fall,

"man cannot turn and prepare himself, by his own natural strength and works, to faith, and calling upon God because human beings have no power to do good works, pleasant and acceptable to God, without the grace of God by Christ preventing us, that we may have a good will, and working with us, when we have that good will."[38]

In surveying the continuity, Matthew Pinson points out that not all who call themselves Arminians affirm total depravity. Still, most do, and traditional Wesleyans are close in line on the issue of corruption and inability. The Wesleyan writer Timothy Tennent affirms that "we are dead in trespasses and sins and cannot help or assist ourselves. We are totally void of any ability to save ourselves...spiritually dead people have no capacity to respond."[39] One last example can be found in Leroy Forline's *Classical Arminianism*. In this work, Forlines presents the following,

Total Depravity

"It is clear that sin has placed man under condemnation...It is clear that fallen man cannot please God and has no fellowship with God...It is clear that man cannot come to God without the drawing power of the Holy Spirit. It is clear that a work so drastic as to be called a new birth is required for man's salvation."[40]

He spends some time discussing what total depravity is not similar to what we outlined before: it is not that people are unable to do good things. It is not that human beings have no conscience, nor that people indulge in every form of sin or in any sin to the greatest possible extent. Total depravity is not an absolute depravity wherein every person turns into a Hitler, but instead that sinful inclinations condition every aspect of one's being.[41]

"In summary, total means that the corruption has extended to all aspects of man's nature, to his entire being; and depravity means that, because of that corruption, there is nothing man can do to merit saving favor with God."[42]

When speaking on the freedom of the will, in light of the Fall, Forlines explains,

"Before Adam and Eve sinned, it was in the framework of possibilities within which they operated to remain in the practice of complete righteousness, or to commit sin. After they sinned, it no longer remained within the framework of possibilities for them to practice uninterrupted righteousness. The same is true for fallen man now. If anyone understands freedom of the will to mean that an unconverted person could practice righteousness and not sin, he misunderstands the meaning of freedom of the will for fallen human beings. Romans 8:7-8 makes it clear that scripture does not teach this.[43]

Appealing to John 6, Forlines says that man cannot respond to the gospel unless the Holy Spirit draws them.[44]

We will pause the discussion here so that we don't go beyond the essential point of this section: *Arminianism proper holds to total depravity and total inability along with Calvinists.* Not only this, but Arminianism historically rejects Pelagianism and semi-Pelagianism. The adherence to original sin dismisses the former, and the commitment to total inability rejects the latter. While there is a difference between Calvinists and Arminians on how the mechanics of the human will work in the bigger picture, Arminians believe man cannot be saved until grace first repairs the will. Man is unable to be saved without a special internal grace. Man is only free to be sinful in his fallen state.[45]

We will discuss the bigger picture of the human will in the next chapter, but for now, we will address the Calvinist's articulation of total depravity in brief.

Calvinism on Total Depravity

The Calvinist view of total depravity does not need much time spent on it as it is a well-known position that also agrees with much of what has been said already. Regardless, I believe presenting some documentation on the subject will be helpful, especially regarding the will. Beginning with the Canons of Dort, the third point of doctrine, article 1, discusses the effect of the fall on human nature,

> "Man was originally created in the image of God and was furnished in his mind with a true and salutary knowledge of his creator and things spiritual, in his will and heart with righteousness, and in all his emotions with purity; indeed, the whole man was holy. However, rebelling against God at the devil's instigation and by his own free will, he deprived himself of these outstanding gifts. Rather, in their place he brought upon himself blindness, terrible darkness, futility, and distortion of judgment in his mind; perversity, defiance, and hardness in his heart and will; and finally, impurity in all his emotions."

Article 2 of the third point of doctrine points out that this corruption spreads to all of the decedents of Adam, while article 3 states,

> "all people are conceived in sin and are born children of wrath, unfit for any saving good, inclined to evil, dead

in their sins, and slaves to sin; without the grace of the regeneration Holy Spirit they are neither willing nor able to return to God, to reform their distorted nature, or even to dispose themselves to such reform."

This sentiment is contained in both the Westminster Confession of Faith and the London Baptist Confession. Quoting chapter 6.3-4 from the London Baptist Confession of Faith, we read,

"They (Adam and Eve) being the root, and by God's appointment, standing in the room and stead of all mankind, the guilt of the sin was imputed, and corrupted natured conveyed, to all their posterity descending from them by ordinary generation, being now conceived in sin, and by nature children of wrath, the servants of sin, the subjects of death, and all other miseries, spiritual, temporal, and eternal, unless the Lord Jesus set them free. From this original corruption, whereby we are utterly indisposed, disable, and made opposite to all good, and wholly incline to all evil, do proceed all actual transgression."

It is from our corrupt nature that all sin proceeds, and humanity does not accidentally commit a sin, nor is sin a passing affliction on man. Man lives out of their sinful nature. The sinful tree bears sinful fruit, which cannot be corrected without the intervention of divine grace. As I gave some ground to the Arminian position before, I want to briefly mention that Calvinism does not deny human agency or, if one wants to say, "free will." Instead, Calvinists will posit that the human will is free insomuch as its nature allows it to be. This becomes particularly important in our subsequent discussion on incompatibilism and compatibilism.

Summary

When it comes to the effect of the fall on human nature, Calvinists and Classical Arminians find general agreement. Classical Arminians, in fact, often lament those who claim the title of Arminian yet reject the necessity of prevenient grace and the reality of total depravity. The divergences between the two views will become more apparent when we discuss the human will in a broader sense and how it is understood in the context of prevenient grace and eternal security. While both positions recognize that man is in bondage to sin, can choose nothing but that which is sinful, and cannot be saved apart from saving grace, they differ on how they understand man's will as it pertains to the larger picture concerning God's sovereignty. The next chapter will be challenging, but it is one of the critical components that ripples through each system and demonstrates a fundamental point of contention between the two positions.

WHAT TOTAL DEPRAVITY IS NOT:

- It is not a rejection of the fact that some sins are worse than others and that some sinners are worse than others.
- It is not a claim that all people are as sinful as they could possibly be.
- It is not a claim that our humanity is gone or that the image of God was forfeited.

Total Depravity

- It is not a claim that humans cannot do good deeds, but rather that man can do no spiritual good.

WHAT TOTAL DEPRAVITY IS:

- Depravity refers to the damaged relationship between God and mankind and the corruption of the human nature which leads to an ongoing inclination towards sin.
- Total refers to the extent and comprehensiveness of the effects of sin.
- In other words: the effects of the fall extend to every dimension of human existence - all parts of men (heart, mind, will, desires) are sinful - all of man is affected, it is *total*.

Chapter 3
The Human Will

So far, we have discussed the human will as it relates to the sinful nature of man taken on because of the fall of Adam. We have also learned that Calvinism and Arminianism find agreement on the total inability. Man is unable to respond to the gospel apart from a special work of grace whereby the human will is repaired and made able to respond. While differing conceptions of that grace can affect how one views the depravity of man, we are first going to focus on the big picture of the human will. This means looking at the human will in the narrative of scripture. What is 'free will' even in a state of a corrupt human nature, and how does it work with God's sovereignty?

This broader definition will ultimately impact the differences between Calvinism and Arminianism on nearly every other point. Unfortunately, the debate is often reduced to "free will" vs. "predestination." This is reductionistic, as Arminians do not believe in the free will of man that is often placed upon him (see Chapter 2), nor do they neglect predestination. Likewise, Calvinists formally do not ignore the freedom of the will or predestination. Both systems affirm both ideas, yet it is a matter of *how* those ideas work themselves out that becomes the point of contention.

With this said, it is worth pointing out that *both systems* face problems that often end up being left to mystery. This is important to keep in mind, lest we overstate the issues of one approach over another. There are tensions in both understandings, and ultimately, we have to think through which of them account for the Biblical data more faithfully. Additionally, while Calvinists and Arminians understand human freedom differently, they agree that human beings possess a level of personal freedom that separates them from the rest of the created order, make numerous important choices, and are conscious willing people who are not robotic products of outside forces.

We must now discuss the spectrum that divides the Calvinist and Arminian on human will, which will logically move us into the topic of God's sovereignty and foreknowledge. A brief definition of the various positions and a minor detour is in order before we proceed.

There are two broad pictures concerning the human will: incompatibilism and compatibilism. Compatibilism, or soft determinism, holds that divine determinism is compatible with human freedom – this is the Calvinist position we will expand on. Determinism is the notion that prior conditions necessarily and causally determine all things that occur in the world and given those specific prior conditions: there is only one outcome. Incompatibilism says the opposite: Determinism is incompatible with human freedom. Arminians fall into the position of incompatibilism, adhering to libertarian free will, also called libertarianism. This should not be confused with the political position and will be discussed more as we proceed. Libertarian free will is not the only form of incompatibilism, as hard determinism would also fall into this category. Hard determinism is the view that all choices are causally determined, and this determinism is incompatible with human freedom and responsibility.

The Spectrum on the Human Will in Ancient Judaism

Many times in discussions, it is asserted that the position of compatibilism did not exist until Augustine. It is further argued that the early church was decisively libertarian. While we conceded early on that they spoke a lot about free agency or free will, it was also said that the way they viewed the finer details regarding God's sovereignty and its relationship to the human will is difficult to ascertain. This is particularly true when we consider how they will cite Pauline texts on predestination and election without further explanation. This means that ultimately, we will always need to go to the Bible, in order to settle the issue.

While libertarianism is often assumed, it should not be adopted so quickly on the assumptions mentioned above. People often think that it was the only view in the Ancient Jewish world, which is incorrect. Literature has shown sufficiently that the positions of determinism, compatibilism, and libertarian free will were all present during the New Testament period.[1] Klawans outlines the ancient Jewish historian Josephus' explanation of the Jews' position of his day, while also providing a nuanced understanding of compatibilism amongst the Pharisees.[2] To this day, Second Temple literature such as Ben Sira, a piece of wisdom literature highly popular amongst the Jews in Jesus' day, is debated about its precise position on the matter. Yet, the work shows that the issues were up for debate and appears to favor compatibilism.

The three major sects in Judaism have traditionally

The Human Will

been understood to hold to the following positions: The Essenes holding to determinism (though they still spoke about free will), the Pharisees holding to various forms of compatibilism, and the Sadducees holding to libertarian freedom, denying the predestination of any event altogether.[3] Robert Wiesner explains how predestinarian election was present in the era, and argues for its relevance in Pauline theology because of Paul's position as a Pharisee before coming to Christ, as well as what appears to be influence from Essene literature.[4] Wiesner will be revisited in chapter six, but Michelle Lee-Barnewall summarizes,

> "Although the Pharisees believed in divine providence, according to Josephus, they also held that the ability to do what was right or wrong was within the capacity of every person, so that fate cooperated with human free will. Thus, according to Josephus, they held to a position in between the Essenes, who believed that all events are ascribed to God's will and the Sadducees, who rejected fate entirely."[5]

This is ultimately to say that the views we are discussing were present at the time of Jesus, albeit without the information provided in the New Testament documents, as they had not been written yet. Furthermore, the positions as they were in the Second Temple period were not necessarily in the refined forms of later centuries. Indeed, Augustine's conception cannot be assumed any more than libertarianism can be, but we are unable to dismiss compatibilism on the grounds that

"Augustine invented it," a common argument in current discussions. Perhaps he refined or modified it, but it already existed. The relevance here should be obvious. We cannot merely assume the early church held to one position or another. We must go back to the text and find the position that best accounts for the scriptural data. We also cannot attribute a position to an individual who appears later in church history as if they invented it.

Arminians and Libertarian Free Will

Matthew Pinson begins his explanation of what Arminians believe about free will with the following,

> "If traditional Arminians do not affirm the semi-Pelagian account of free will, what do they mean when they say they believe in free will in salvation. In short, they mean freedom from necessity, not freedom from depravity."[6]

Pointing to Arminius, Pinson states that the "key to his doctrine of free will was his differentiation of necessity, contingency, and certainty."[7] He explains that the contingent things are not required to turn out the way they, in fact, will. In other words, they have the possibility to go any direction. There are multiple potential outcomes. Necessary things must turn out the way they will – there is no possibility of the contrary outcome. Jacob Arminius believed for an act to be free, it had to be a contingency. "It has to have been able to go one of two or more ways."[8]

> "Thus, Arminius agreed with the idea that is known as 'libertarian freedom.' This is freedom, not from the power of sin or depravity, but from necessity. God has created his universe in such a way as to maintain creaturely freedom."[9]

This means that while man is fallen and a slave to sin, he is always free to choose from multiple possible outcomes in his day-to-day actions while being unable to choose God without an internal movement of grace. At conversion, when grace repairs and frees the man's will from the bondage of sin, man can then choose to either take hold of faith or resist grace. This notion of freedom from necessity – a fixed outcome – becomes the basis for resistible grace while still limiting man's freedom in total depravity before grace works in man to respond to the gospel.

Jerry Walls and Joseph Dongell explain in their work, Why I am Not A Calvinist, that the view of libertarian freedom maintains that choices are undetermined. There is a process of deliberation that presupposes the reality that it is up to us to decide and that "it seems intuitively and immediately evident that many of our actions are up to us in the sense that when faced with a decision, both or more options are within our power to choose."[10] Roger Olson states that, "Free agency is the ability to do the other than what one in fact does."[11]

Thus, Human beings can make choices contrary to the choices they actually make – they have the power of contrary choice. Furthermore, the choices that are made are not determined by anything outside the person making the choices – there is no sufficient condition or cause for the choice in question. For the libertarian, this does not reject the reality of influences and reasons for a choice, such as values, motivations, preferences. Rather, they believe the will can overrule all these factors. Leroy Forlines explains that,

> "The freedom of the will does not mean that forces or influences cannot be brought to bear on the will. In fact,

the very nature of freedom of the will means that forces or influences will be brought to bear on the will. It does not mean that these forces cannot be a contributing factor in the exercise of the will. It does mean that these influences or forces cannot guarantee or determine the action of the will."[12]

Compatibilist, Christensen states about the position,

"In most cases, compelling reasons might appeal to a person, who then chooses to follow its leading. What cannot happen is that a set of reasons becomes "strong enough to move the [person] decisively to choose one thing over another. Even if a person agrees in light of various reasons and arguments presented that one course of action is preferable, that in no way guarantees that it must be followed." Free will means that we always have alternative choices at our disposal and that we exercise complete control over which alternative we choose. Christian libertarians believe that God endows his creatures with this freedom and that he steadfastly refuses to interfere with it except in rare cases."[13]

In the same vein on the topic of influences, Libertarians accept the reality that people cannot do literally whatever they want. Humanity is limited as human beings with human limitations, and a person's character and circumstances will further influence one's decisions.

To the libertarian, this position, the ability to choose to the contrary, is critical for ensuring the responsibility of the creature and is the only proper way to understand creaturely freedom. Olson will argue,

> "Arminians believe in free will because they see it everywhere assumed in the Bible, and because it is necessary to protect God's reputation...the real reason Arminians reject divine control of every human choice and action is that this would make God the author of sin and evil. For Arminians this makes God at least morally ambiguous and at worst the only sinner."[14]

For passages that Calvinists appeal to because they teach "strong divine sovereignty," Arminians will state that they do not indicate God "necessitates all human choices and events and that people have no choice but to do what they do by necessity."[15] The libertarian believes those scriptural texts that present a command or a choice for the individual presuppose libertarian free will – the power of contrary choice. For example, texts such as "choose this day whom you will serve" in Joshua 24:15 are evoked to show this presupposition.

Furthermore, texts that implore individuals to come to God, such as the famous John 3:16, follow suit. Additionally, texts where God has appeared to change his mind are presented, indicating that the course of the future is changing, such as Exodus 32:9-14. Matthew 23:37 is cited as well as Jesus laments over Jerusalem because of the Jews' resistance to his message. In addition to this, verses that indicate that God does "not wish that any should perish but that all should reach repentance" (2 Peter 3:9) and that God "desires all people to be saved and to come to the knowledge of the truth" (1 Timothy 2:4) demonstrate to the libertarian that God does not always see his desires fulfilled, but instead has created a world where humans operate in libertarian free will.

Essentially, libertarianism's support from Biblical texts are those that refer to or assume human agency. Because human experience leads itself to view the world through free agency and the power to choose to the contrary, libertarianism is often assumed. Some summary points of the libertarian position are: If our love for God is determined, it cannot have meaningful value; blame or praise is only meaningful when a person can act contrary. Obligations and commands imply that we can obey, and libertarianism keeps God from being the author or culpable for sin and evil. The libertarian believes their position better answers the problem of evil (called theodicy) and the human experience.

The logical question that follows is how do Arminians understand God's sovereignty and foreknowledge? The libertarian will need to explain how God's plan and the unfolding of history occur in light of their position. Further, we need to see how foreknowledge, which is God's knowledge of all events past, present, future, works itself out in the libertarian scheme if humans have the power of contrary choice at any crossroad.

Arminians and Sovereignty

I'll rely heavily on Olson and Pinson when examining the Arminian position on sovereignty and foreknowledge. This is because this presentation on sovereignty and foreknowledge is not the only understanding in the Arminian model. There are a number of internal discussions within Arminian circles regarding the role of middle knowledge, or Molinism, and its compatibility with Arminianism. It would be good to seek out and consult Arminians on those discussions, as here we will focus on Olson and Pinson, who present what is called simple foreknowledge. Beginning with Pinson he states,

> "In scripture, a sovereign – even an absolute sovereign – is someone who extends his rule over his subjects and propounds laws for them to obey. If they do not obey those laws, they are subject to punishment or even banishment from the sovereign's realm. Even an absolute sovereign does not determine his subjects' moment-by-moment lives so that they will be guaranteed to carry out his will."[16]

Pinson, citing the Lutheran, Hans Martensen, points out that

> "God limits his own power by calling into existence…a world of created beings to whom he gives in a derivative way to have life in themselves. But precisely in this way above all other – that he is omnipotent over a free world – does he reveal the inner greatness of his power more clearly. That is true power which brings free agents into existence and is not withstanding able to make itself all in all."[17]

This view of sovereignty is compared to a man who is

in control of his family by ensuring that everyone follows the established rules. There is no determination of every act in reality. Pinson goes on to state that the universe is not characterized by random chance, but that he can find agreement with Calvinist Louis Berkhof when he describes that God is clothed with absolute authority, upholds all things with his power, and determines the ends which they are destined to serve.[18] Further, Pinson says,

> "Arminians can even agree with Berkhof that 'He rules as king in the most absolute sense of the word, and all things are dependent on him and subservient to him.' As Arminian theologian Kevin Hester states, 'God's sovereignty is such a clear biblical teaching that no biblical conscious Christian would dare assail it. The question is whether, and if so in what way, human freedom coexists with God's sovereign plan and control of the universe."[19]

The Arminian will say that God still governs all things, allows the freedom of choice of human beings, and draws those humans into his plans for his ends. Pinson says, "God governs the world to his desired ends while still maintaining creaturely freedom. He permits evil yet does not ordain it."[20] Arminians agree with Calvinists that God's providence over creation is a reality, so much so that if God removed his hand from the world, it would stop moving.

Furthermore, in Jacob Arminius' writings, there is a distinction between two modes of God's will: God's antecedent will and consequent will. God's antecedent will is the will and pleasure that comes from God himself. The consequent will of God is his will of permission. To put it another way,

> "God's antecedent will involves those things that God approvingly wills. His consequent will involves those things that he merely allows. Without God's grace we can do nothing good. Yet our actions are free in the sense of libertarian free will."[21]

Roger Olson follows along the same line. Olson states,

> "Faithful followers of Arminius have always believed that God governs the entire universe and all of history. Nothing at all can happen without God's permission, and many things are specifically and directly controlled and caused by God. Even sin and evil do not escape God's providential governance in Classical Arminian theology. God permits and limits them without willing or causing them."[22]

He continues to point out that, for Arminians, God allows human freedom of choice and then responds by drawing them into his plan for his ends.[23] Olson is most concerned with avoiding the notion that God is the author of sin and evil. He believes Arminianism avoids this issue in that the agency of human beings is allowed, and God permits evil to occur rather than ordains it. Also, evil must be permitted by God if it occurs; it cannot happen if God does not allow it.

The Human Will

"God has the ability to stop anything from happening, but to preserve human liberty he permits sin and evil without approving them."[24]

Further,

"God permits it designedly and willingly, but not efficaciously. Furthermore, God controls (ordains, appoints, limits, directs) it in a sense that he points it to a good end."[25]

Olson, when describing Jacob Arminius on the subject explains,

"God is the first cause of whatever happens; even a sinful act cannot occur without God as its first cause, because creatures have no ability to act without their creator, who is their supreme cause for existence" and when a sinful act occurs, "the same event is produced by God and the human being, the guilt of the sin is not transferred to God, because God is the effecter of the acts but only the permitter of the sin itself. This is why scripture sometimes attributes evil deeds to God; because God concurs with them. God cooperates with the sinners who commit them. But that does not mean that God is the efficacious cause of them or wills them, except according to his consequent will. God allows them and cooperates with them unwillingly in order preserve the sinners liberty."[26]

God wills to permit sin and supports it without

approval, which requires a prior self-limitation of God. The question then becomes, how do Arminians understand God's foreknowledge, which is the reality that God knows all things and has always known all things? This point becomes crucial as we consider God's attribute of omniscience; he knows all things possible, and no knowledge escapes God.

Arminians and Foreknowledge

Within Classical Arminianism, there are two kinds of events: contingent events, that is, events that could have been otherwise, and necessary events which could not have been otherwise (or predetermined events). Necessary events were foreordained, but others can turn out one way or another. Foreordination simply means that God ordained, ordered, or decreed something to occur. In the Arminian picture, both of these necessary and contingent events are present in history and are as God designed them to be. Pinson posits the issue of divine foreknowledge as this,

> "How can an event be free if God knows it is going to come to pass? If God's knowledge is true, does it not make the event certain? Therein lies the explanation. A future event can be certain without being necessary."[27]

An event can happen one way or another without it forfeiting God's certainty that the event will go in a particular direction. God's certainty of an event does not mean that it is predetermined or caused by God. Pinson uses this illustration,

> "If I decide to go crappie fishing at the lake tomorrow morning, God knows that and has always known that. Yet the reason he has always known it is that he knows everything truly and exhaustively. However, if I freely choose instead to go to the donut shop tomorrow rather than the lake, then God instead knows that and has always known it. So if, in eternity past, God knew that I would go fishing at 7:00 a.m. tomorrow, then it is certain that I will do so, but it is not necessary. The only reason God knew that I would go is because of my choice to go. My will was the cause of my action, not God's knowledge. Things are caused by other things than knowledge of them, whether divine or human."[28]

The Classical Arminian thinks,

> "What God knew yesterday is contingent upon what I will freely decide to do tomorrow. If I am free to decide whether to do something or refrain from it, it is up to me to decide which I shall do; and whichever I decide to do, God will have known yesterday, and indeed, from eternity, that I will do it.'"[29]

However, Pinson admits that the understanding of how God's foreknowledge works in Arminianism differs among Arminians. Arminians are generally much more diverse in how they discuss foreknowledge compared to Calvinists.

Calvinists and Compatibilism

Having looked at the Arminian picture of the human will, God's sovereignty, and foreknowledge, we can now move on to the Calvinist position. I'll be presenting the common position of soft determinism or compatibilism. Many argue that this is the classical Calvinist position, though a minority will say that hard determinism is the norm. There are also others who limit the deterministic aspects of compatibilism to only soteriology (predestination, election, etc.), while holding to a libertarian freedom of the will in general. Like Arminianism, there is some diversity in Calvinistic circles to be found. Furthermore, like Arminianism, there are eventually levels of mystery as you continue down the rabbit hole.

We will begin this topic by discussing human freedom in Calvinism. Like libertarianism, Calvinism teaches that human beings are real free agents in the world and will always choose from various options. At the same time, Calvinists disagree with libertarianism regarding God's role in these choices and even other influences' degree of influence on a person's choices. The axiom of libertarianism - that man can choose otherwise than all his inclinations and motives - is denied in the Calvinistic understanding of the human will. Calvinists insist that man will always choose according to his nature and greatest desire, even when he appears not to desire his choice. To illustrate this point, consider a man who must choose between a salad and pizza. While he may want the pizza more on the surface, he chooses his less ideal salad option because his desire to be healthy is stronger than his desire for pizza.

The difference between libertarianism and compatibilism regarding human freedom is that in libertarianism, the will is the free force, and there is a tendency to neglect that the person is the one who operates within the will. Calvinists will say that libertarians do not adequately maintain the reality that various factors drive people and their choices. John Frame states,

> "We act and speak, then, according to our character. We follow the deepest desires of our heart. To my knowledge, Scripture never refers to this moral consistency as a kind of freedom, but the concept of heart-act consistency is important in Scripture, and theologians and philosophers have often referred to it as freedom. In everyday life, we regularly think of freedom as doing what we want to do. When we don't do what we want, we are either acting irrationally or being forced to act against our will by someone or something thing outside ourselves.
>
> This kind of freedom is sometimes called compatibilism, because it is compatible with determinism. Determinism is the view that every event (including human actions) has a sufficient cause other than itself. Compatibilist freedom means that even if every act we perform is caused by something outside ourselves (such as natural causes or God), we are still free, for we can still act according to our character and desires."[30]

The actions of the individual are actions that they freely want and desire to make. Our acts result from our will, and our person influences our will. Just as libertarians recognize the limitations of human nature, like the fact that we cannot naturally choose to breathe underwater, so do the Calvinists. We make choices that are consistent with our nature and all of the complexities that come with our person. Just as God's will is limited to his nature and character, and thus he will not sin, humans are limited to their nature as creatures.[31] Contrary to libertarianism, the Calvinist believes the will is not self-determining but driven by the person making the choice, and freedom is being able to act and choose according to that which one desires. There is no constraining what that individual desires to do. In the Calvinist position, "People possess this freedom because God has created us as moral, free agents."[32] Chapter 9 of the London Baptist Confession of Faith opens with this,

> "God hath endued the will of man, with that natural liberty, and power of acting upon choice; that it is neither forced, nor by any necessity of nature determined to do good or evil."

The will has the natural liberty to act in accordance with its nature, and acts on choice; it can choose between different courses. Further, this will is neither forced nor determined to be either good or evil. Man was created with a will that can do either good or evil. The following sections of the Baptist confession would describe the fall of man and the radical change of man's nature wherein man would lose the ability to will any spiritual good accompanying salvation. Yet, even after the fall, man is still free to act per his nature.

With the free agency of man and the Calvinist understanding of human will put forward, we can now continue on to compatibilism. Compatibilism is a belief that holds two positions in tension, which Wright summarizes,

> "1) God is absolutely sovereign, but in his sovereignty never functions in a way that human responsibility is curtailed, minimized, or mitigated and 2) Human beings are morally responsible creatures – they significantly choose, rebel, obey, believe, defy, make decisions and so forth, and they are rightly held accountable for those action; but this characteristic never functions as to make God absolutely contingent, meaning dependent on something outside himself."[33]

Thus, compatibilism holds in tension that God is absolutely sovereign, but people are genuinely free agents responsible for their actions and choices. Peterson and Williams point out,

> "The Calvinist notion of divine sovereignty is often portrayed as little more than a theological gloss upon a doctrine of philosophical determinism. But this misses the Calvinist point, and certainly misses the biblical witness to the sovereignty of God. The providential and sovereign power of God is neither an abstract nor a

distant force; rather, through personal power God effects his will in the world."[34]

And,

> "The error of identifying divine sovereignty with determinism or fatalism comes from the abstraction of the issue into impersonal terms. Divine sovereignty is not a blind and deterministic force any more than God himself is some impersonal it. The same is true when we speak of human freedom and accountability. It is our freedom and responsibility."[35]

Peterson and Williams are further helpful in underlining that God is lord over his creation, which includes the freedom and responsibility of human beings. Still, as creatures, we are never given freedom from God, he is God. Instead, we are given a freedom of creaturely existence.[36] In compatibilism, God's determination of his plans to come to pass includes the free choices and actions of human beings – God is an active agent of history who is able to ensure that his will is fulfilled. Peterson and Williams state,

> "Neither does God's sovereignty make human beings mindless pawns or exonerate them of responsibility for their choices and actions, nor do human responsibility and freedom frustrate God's ability to realize his will. Scripture teaches both that God is always the sovereign king over his creation and that human beings are always accountable for their actions. Both are assumed as true

throughout the biblical record, and neither is seen as limiting the other. Paul Helm goes so far as to speak of divine sovereignty and human responsibility as "fixed points" within the biblical drama."[37]

Chapter 5 of the London Baptist Confession of Faith on providence, section 2, points out,

> "Although in relation to the foreknowledge and decree of God, the first cause, all things come to pass immutably and infallibly; so that there is not anything, befalls any by chance or without his providence; yet by the same providence he orders them to fall out, according to the nature of second causes, either necessarily, freely, or contingently."

By God's decree, wisdom, and knowledge, all things occur with purpose but "according to the nature of second causes, either necessarily, freely, or contingently." God is the first cause, but his will is worked through second causes. The word "necessarily" here points to things such as order settled in nature, such as laws of the universe. "Freely" points to the moral actions of the rational creature, i.e., man.[38] Regarding sin, section 4 of the confession states that God's providence extends itself to sinful actions

> "The Almighty power, unsearchable wisdom, and infinite goodness of God, so far manifest themselves in his Providence, that his determinate Councel extendeth it self even to the first fall, and all other sinful actions both

of Angels, and Men; (and that not by a bare permission) which also he most wisely and powerfully boundeth, and otherwise ordereth, and governeth, in a manifold dispensation to his most holy ends: yet so, as the sinfulness of their acts proceedeth only from the Creatures, and not from God; who being most holy and righteous, neither is nor can be, the author or approver of sin."

While they are similar,[39] Arminianism believes that it is by bare permission that these acts occur rather than by decree. In the London Baptist Confession, the concept of bare permission is rejected. According to Arminianism, God does not will these actions except by his consequent will. Thus, he still willed to permit the actions passively.

Calvinism affirms that God uses secondary causes and is still the first cause, same as the Arminian. Calvinism likewise rejects that God is the author or approver of sin. Yet, Calvinists would argue that God is not passively permitting evil, which indeed is what he still wills in Arminianism, just for the sake of libertarian freedom. Instead, he has these actions actively serving his purposes. While the Arminian can say that these permissions are for God's purposes, God is ultimately needing to react to the free choices of men, which takes precedence in God's prior self-limitation.

As the LBCF expressed, God is not the author or approver of sin. Sinful actions flow from the sinful nature of the creatures. God has no part in committing the sin in the same way Arminius claimed above. Calvinists will point out that both positions thus affirm that God allows or permits evil, yet in the libertarian model, it is a passive allowance rather than a providential or active decree of permission. Further, this passive allowance is not only logically less guided, thus lacking meaningful and ultimate good purpose at its occurrence, but it does not solve the problem of evil. Both positions have the human acting and being culpable as the secondary cause.

Compatibilists have historically pointed to the narrative of Joseph (beginning in Genesis 37) to explain how God can ordain evil without being culpable for evil or evil intentions. In Joseph's narrative, we find that his brothers had evil intentions in their dealings with him. They wanted to get rid of him and acted against Joseph, selling him into slavery and lying to their father about his fate (Genesis 37:18-33). Following his time in Egypt, which began with hardship but ended with his role as prime minister, Joseph is reunited with his brothers. In this reunion, Joseph states that both his brothers and God sent him to Egypt (Genesis 45:4-5; 8), and later he points out that while his brothers intended evil against him, God intended those same actions for good (Genesis 50:20).

We have what Christensen labels as a dual explanation for what occurred.[40] When we answer the question of who acted in Joseph's life, we can state that it was both his brothers and God. The brother's actions are sinful, with evil intent, and yet God's actions are with good intent. Both parties were involved, yet Joseph's brothers are guilty due to their malicious intent and resulting actions.

While the discussions on the freedom of the will in these positions are often centered around the problem of evil, the Calvinist argues that libertarianism does not solve the issue. It remains a tension in the Christian ethic regardless of your tradition. The Calvinist goes on to critique the Arminian framework where libertarian freedom is of greater value than preventing evil. How so? In libertarianism, God is sufficiently powerful to stop anything from happening, but he doesn't always because of libertarian free will. In fact, we must ask why God prevents or hinders any evil at all if libertarian freedom is so essential.

Further, when God does permit evil, it is senseless and without purpose as it is ultimately to uphold a creature's freedom of will and may not be necessary for the events in God's plan. As Christensen illustrates, it is as if there is a police officer who stands by while a homeless man is being beaten to death when he could stop it but cannot because it would violate the perpetrator's free will.[41] Both systems have tensions on this level, and it is an inescapable mystery where the lesson of Job comes into play for the Christian, as it pertains to suffering.

Arminianism is based on the texts of scripture that speak to humans making choices along with the assumption of incompatibilism. For the Compatibilist, the free agency of human beings occurs in tension with strong providential sovereignty. How does the Compatibilist defend this via the text?

They find the human free agency texts utilized by Arminians appropriate to their position as it holds in tension sovereignty and free agency. There is a dual explanation for actions, some clear and others not. To demonstrate this, Calvinists look at examples of God and man moving simultaneously in the same events. However, before moving to those free agency texts, compatibilism

The Human Will

begins with sovereignty texts because of God's prerogative as sovereign lord. This is stressed by texts such as Proverbs 16:9, where we read that the "heart of man plans his way, but the Lord establishes his steps." This sentiment is found in other Proverbs, such as 19:21, which states, "many are the plans in the mind of a man, but it is the purpose of the Lord that will stand." Others to consider are Proverbs 20:24 and 21:1. Sawn D. Wright lists the following texts on this point of sovereignty:

- "See now that I, even I, am he, and there is no god beside me; I kill and I make alive; I wound and I heal; and there is none that can deliver out of my hand. (Deut. 32:39)
- The Lord does whatever pleases him, in the heavens and on the earth, in the seas and all their depths. (Ps. 135:6)
- Your eyes saw my unformed substance; in your book were written, every one of them, the days that were formed for me, when as yet there were none of them. (Ps. 139:16)
- I form light and create darkness, I make well-being and create calamity, I am the Lord, who does all these things. (Isa. 45:7)
- [God] works all things according to the counsel of his will. (Eph. 1:11)"[42]

Calvinists then consider the texts of human agency that demonstrate dual agency. As mentioned before, a prominent example is found in the narrative surrounding Joseph. In this narrative, we see God and Joseph's brothers moving simultaneously, with different intentions and the same outcome. Joseph says that both God and his brothers sent him to Egypt, but most importantly, Joseph in Genesis 50:20 proclaims that what his brothers *intended* for evil, God had *intended* for good.

The Compatibilist often points to several other examples of dual agency in the text. For example, Calvinists will note that the Assyrians decided to invade Israel, yet God says that Assyria is his agent in bringing punishment upon Israel in Isaiah 10:5-12. The text indicates that it was God who sent the Assyrians and who wreaked havoc against Israel. Still, the Assyrians are held accountable and responsible for their actions, their arrogance, and their thirst for blood.

Compatibilists will also argue from the narratives of Pharaoh's hardened heart, the Sons of Eli, Jonah, and other events, but three examples stand out. The first centers around Judas Iscariot's betrayal of Jesus, which is indicated to be foreknown by God and part of the fulfillment of scripture. Judas is not only held responsible for his freely chosen actions to betray Jesus (seen in texts such as Matthew 26:14-16) but he is said to have been influenced by Satan's entrance into him (Luke 22:3-6), while he was also chosen by Jesus himself (John 6:70; 17:12), all of which was the fulfillment of the divine plan (Matthew 26:24; Mark 14:21).

This tension is elevated when we consider Satan's role in the life of Job, particularly in chapter 1. Notice that in Job's narrative, there are three major agents in his suffering. First, Satan challenged God and would afflict Job. Second, God allowed Satan to bring suffering to Job, and lastly, people groups attacked him. Each intent was different, yet the same outcome occurred - Job's suffering.

Back to the narrative of Judas, we find full culpability for Judas' actions with multiple agents at play. However, Judas ultimately leads to the Compatibilist's other example, which is Christ's crucifixion. All theologians have recognized that the crucifixion of Christ was not an accident but rather a planned event. Yet, the event is surrounded by the will of many individuals and agents, some of whom were later called out for their culpability at Pentecost. When speaking on this point, Peterson and Williams state,

> "Now if God ordained that the crucifixion of Jesus would take place, we must say that Judas, Pilate and the others were not free in the libertarian sense of absolute power to choose the contrary. Judas could not have not betrayed Jesus. Herod and the Jews could not have chosen not to be murderous. Does this mean then that they were not free? If they acted according to the purpose of God, were they manipulated as if they were no more than pawns? That is the inCompatibilist contention, but Scripture nowhere suggests such an inference. God did not ordain the actions of Herod or Pilate as if they were puppets. None of those involved in the death of Jesus acted contrary to their wills or in violation of their character. They did as they chose to do. Jesus was crucified because Judas, Herod, Pilate and the others conspired to kill him. Their choices were part of God's eternal plan, but that fact did not remove one bit of human accountability. Divine sovereignty and

human responsibility cannot be pitted against one another."[43]

Not only is this an event that shows the compatibility between sovereignty and the human will, but we find different intentions and motivations at play here similar to the narrative of Joseph and his brothers.

A final example before moving on to Calvinism and foreknowledge is the inspiration of scripture. Theologically, Christians have upheld the doctrine of the verbal inspiration of the Bible. This states that the Bible is God's word yet has human authorship. Further, Christians have generally rejected the dictation theory of inspiration as it would eliminate or fail to account for the authentic and obvious 'flavors' of the Bible's diverse human authorship.

When we confess the Word of God as being written by humans led by the Holy Spirit, there is a Compatibilist understanding of agency. The role of the Holy Spirit did not remove the human agency necessary for the outcome. Christensen, on this point, asks whether or not it would be possible for Paul to write something contrary to God under the inspiration of the Holy Spirit, and answers of course not![44] Paul wrote freely, in accordance with his concerns and in his own unique style, that which God intended to have penned in scripture. Christensen presses on the issue,

> "If one holds to libertarian freedom, it becomes very difficult to see how God guaranteed that the human authors of Scripture would write anything that corresponded to his desires. Maybe they just happened to

write everything he intended, but this is so improbable as to render it virtually impossible. Even if God strongly influenced them to write his divine precepts, they could have always resisted this influence, mixing it with their own contrary thoughts and words. Unless God causally determines the words of Scripture in some way, it seems that one is inevitably led to a defective view of Scripture's revelation, inspiration, and inerrancy and its infallible conveyance of divine truth."[45]

Calvinists and Foreknowledge

As with Arminians, Calvinists rightly agree that God knows everything. Further, he always knows all things and never increases in knowledge as God is all-knowing and immutable. The distinction between Calvinists and Classical Arminians is this: to Calvinists God knows everything that occurs because he has decreed all that will occur. Foreordination logically comes before foreknowledge – and this 'logical' order must be stressed lest we think of it in terms of time. Curt Daniel says,

> "They [foreordination and foreknowledge] are so close and inseparable that the word foreknow is sometimes used in a causative rather than a cognitive way, as in Acts 2:23. First Peter 1:20 says that Christ was "foreordained before the foundation of the world," and the word is literally foreknown. God did not merely foresee the crucifixion – he predestined it (Acts 4:27-28; Luke 22:22)."[46]

Acts 17:26 speaks briefly on this in that God created humankind through Adam "to live on all the face of the earth, having determined allotted periods and the boundaries of their dwelling place." What God has determined will come to pass, "for what has been determined shall be done" (Daniel 11:36), "To do whatever your hand and your purpose determined before to be done." (Acts 4:28). Because of the differing understanding of foreordination's relationship with foreknowledge, we will find these subjects coming back up when discussing predestination to salvation, particularly with the phrase "those whom God foreknew."

Summary

The picture of the human will in Arminianism allows for the power of contrary choice and ultimately lends itself to resistible grace and conditional election. Libertarianism, which is a category of incompatibilism, posits that man is free from necessity and can find early adherence in the Christian tradition. This position holds God's sovereignty in tension with his pre-self limitations and creaturely freedom while allowing necessary events to occur. Calvinists on the other hand generally hold to compatibilism (soft-determinism) which holds God's absolute sovereignty and man's creaturely freedom in tension. Some Calvinists fall under a category of incompatibilism known as determinism (or hard determinism), but most adhere to soft determinism.

Chapter 4
The Doctrine of Grace

Now that we have spoken to the doctrine of the human will in Calvinism and Arminianism, we can move on to the subject of grace. We have seen that when it comes to total depravity, Arminians and Calvinists find agreement: man without some special grace is not free in his will to come to faith. The Holy Spirit must draw man and free, repair, and strengthen his will first.

However, Calvinism and Arminianism soon begin to separate on a couple of points. Firstly, Arminians express a universal prevenient grace that must be discussed. Secondly, Arminians hold to what is called resistible grace, while Calvinists articulate irresistible grace. Because of libertarianism, the Arminian believes that man can choose to resist grace and not come to Christ when drawn by the Holy Spirit. Grace is resistible. For the Calvinist, however, man will choose not to resist grace and will ultimately come to Christ when drawn by the Holy Spirit. It is irresistible. Those whom God effectually calls will inevitably be converted. In this chapter on grace, we will discuss the conceptions of grace in the Calvinist and Arminian positions and the doctrine of calling.

Grace broadly defined

In an effort to proceed with clarity, I will offer a definition of grace before continuing. Grace is ultimately God's goodness entering into human history and bringing to them undeserved favor. The source of all material and spiritual blessings is God's grace, with subcategories such as common and special grace. The former, common grace, are non-salvific graces seen in God's general care of the world. The latter, which we are concerned with here, is the grace that is the exercise of God's saving power towards the sinner. This grace enlightens the minds of rebels, frees their wills, and energizes their affection toward God. It is an inward work of the Spirit that allows man to willingly believe the gospel, repent of their sins, and trust Christ.

Arminianism and Prevenient Grace

As it has been expressed, Classical Arminianism believes that grace must come before man can respond to the gospel. Jacob Arminius quotes John 6:44 in his work, pointing out that no man can go to the Father unless he is drawn first. The Spirit's prevenient grace must incline the mind and heart towards the gospel for conversion.[1] The Remonstrant declaration follows suit, and so Calvinists and Arminians both uphold a grace that comes before, with the distinction that Arminians believe in a universal grace that is resistible while Calvinists maintain a particular grace that is irresistible grace.[2]

The summaries provided by the Society of Evangelical Arminians are quite helpful on the point of prevenient grace.[3] First, on the general description of the necessity of grace, they state,

> "because human beings are fallen and sinful, they are not able to think, will, nor do anything good in and of themselves, including believe the gospel of Christ (see the description of Total Depravity above). Therefore, desiring the salvation of all and having provided atonement for all people (see "Atonement for All" above), God continues to take the initiative for the purpose of bringing all people to salvation by calling all people everywhere to repent and believe the gospel (Acts 17:30; cf. Matt 28:18-20), and by enabling those who hear the gospel to respond to it positively in faith. Unaided by grace, man cannot even choose to please God or to believe the promise of salvation held out in the gospel.

As Jesus said in John 6:44, "No one can come to me unless the Father who sent me draws him." But thanks be to God, Jesus also promised, "And I, when I am lifted up from the earth, will draw all people to myself" (John 12:32). Thus, the Father and the Son draw all people to Jesus, enabling them to come to Jesus in faith. Even though sinful people are blind to the truth of the gospel (2 Cor 4:4), Jesus came into the world of sinful humanity as "the true light, which enlightens everyone" (John 1:9; cf. 12:36), the light about which John the Baptist came to bear witness, "that all might believe through him" (John 1:7)."[4]

Further,

"All of this is what is known in traditional theological language as God's prevenient grace. The term "prevenient" simply means "preceding." Thus, "prevenient grace" refers to God's grace that precedes salvation, including that part of salvation known as regeneration, which is the beginning of eternal spiritual life granted to all who trust in Christ (John 1:12-13). Prevenient grace is also sometimes called enabling grace or pre-regenerating grace. This is God's unmerited favor toward totally depraved people, who are unworthy of God's blessing and unable to seek God or trust in him in and of themselves. Accordingly, Acts 18:27 indicates that we believe through grace, placing grace preveniently (i.e. logically prior) to faith as the means by which we believe. It is the grace that, among other things, frees our wills to believe in Christ and his gospel. As Titus

2:11 says, "For the grace of God has appeared, bringing salvation for all people."[5]

Here we find the necessity of grace expressed so that man can respond to the gospel and believe in Christ. When it comes to the specifics of what this grace looks like, the Society of Evangelical Arminians are helpful again,

> "Arminians differ among themselves about some of the details of how God's prevenient grace works, probably because Scripture itself does not give a detailed description. Some Arminians believe that God continually enables all people to believe at all times as a benefit of the atonement. Others believe that God only bestows the ability to believe in Christ to people at select times according to his good pleasure and wisdom. Still others believe that prevenient grace generally accompanies any of God's specific movements toward people, rendering them able to respond positively to such movements as God would have them. But all Arminians agree that people are incapable of believing in Jesus apart from the intervention of God's grace and that God does bestow his grace that draws toward salvation on all morally responsible people. With respect to the gospel, seventeenth century Arminian Bishop, Laurence Womack, well said, "on all those to whom the word of faith is preached, the Holy Spirit bestows, or is ready to bestow, so much grace as is sufficient, in fitting degrees, to bring on their conversion."[6]

With this said, we will now summarize some of the points Matthew Pinson brings up about universal prevenient grace, which will assume his particular articulation of grace.

First, Pinson states that prevenient grace should not be confused with natural or general revelation.[7] He points out that while many Arminians tend to conflate the two, it is more appropriate to view prevenient grace "as an individualized drawing which, at one time or another, goes out to all people, in God's own timing and manner."[8] This is to say that prevenient grace is a special grace, not general revelation, i.e., the creation or part of the created order. General revelation is natural, while prevenient grace, or drawing grace of the Holy Spirit, is supernatural. It is the activity of the Holy Spirit.[9]

Secondly, Pinson notes this is a supernatural drawing, not a unilateral lessening of depravity. This is the Holy Spirit working in people's hearts and minds before conversion (Acts 2:37; 10:12; 16:14; 1 Thess. 1:4-5). Classical Arminian Stephen Ashby states that Arminians

> "differ from Wesleyans in our understanding of prevenient grace. It is not like a dense fog settling over a city in which everyone equally shares, hence, canceling out the effects of the Fall for all of humanity. Rather, it is individually directed and brings with it God's enablement as he draws human beings to himself. Though Reformed Arminians insist that God universally provides his salvific grace, they at the same time resist the notion that prevenient grace reverses the effects of the Fall. Rather, such grace, though universal in scope,

acts in enablement and drawing on an individual human level."[10]

Pinson, on this point, says,

> "The Holy Spirit is a person relating to other persons made in his image. Prevenient grace is not a substance one possesses. It is the gracious, enabling influence of the divine person on a human person in a relational dynamic—a back-and-forth, influence-and-response, relational movement. Yet "the Spirit will not always strive with man." This influence, this persuasion, this conviction, this back-and-forth relational experience, is temporary. Like other interpersonal forms of communication and influence, it is something that can come and go."[11]

Third, Pinson is emphatic that this prevenient grace does not mean that people who have never heard the gospel can be saved without the gospel, special revelation, or confessing Christ. He explains this by stating,

> "most Arminians believe that there are two stages of prevenient grace. People receive some motions of prevenient grace before they receive the gospel or special revelation. However, these can never result in salvation. If individuals do not resist the early motions of prevenient grace, they will be given the gospel. This second stage of prevenient grace, which involves the communication of the gospel-word, must occur for individuals to be led to conversion."[12]

The ordinary means and instrument of conversion for many Arminians is the preaching of the word or gospel. When dealing with critiques of Arminianism's prevenient grace, Pinson rejects the notion that the effects of total depravity are neutralized via the cross of Christ. Instead, this is a misunderstanding based on a model that some Wesleyans advocate, but this is not the model of Classical Arminianism. The atonement has not counteracted the effects of Adam's sin so that all people have the opportunity to accept or receive Christ. Instead, God is working personally in individual lives to draw men to the cross and enabling them to respond.

Arminianism and Resistible Grace

We have already noted several passages in our citations of Arminian works that articulate prevenient grace. God's working and drawing all men to himself as the light of the world becomes the basis for this prevenient grace. God's prevenient grace in Arminianism is calling, convicting, wooing, persuading, and enabling people to be his own.

The call of sinners to the gospel is a part of grace wherein man is invited to accept the gospel, and the word of God comes to bear on their heart. However, this call and grace can be resisted. This is connected in part to the issue of libertarian freedom of the will. Man must always have at least two options before him giving him the power of contrary choice. This means that while many individuals will genuinely hear and understand the message of God's grace and have the opportunity to be saved by taking hold of the gift of faith, they will instead resist grace and reject salvation, left on their path to damnation.

There are several texts on the subject of resistible grace that Arminians and others, such as Lutherans, point to. One key text is in Matthew 23:37. In this text, Jesus says,

> "O Jerusalem, Jerusalem, the city that kills the prophets and stones those who are sent to it! How often would I have gathered your children together as a hen gathers her brood under her wings, and you were not willing!"

The Arminian argues that this text demonstrates that Jesus was sincerely and graciously calling people to be his own, and the sole reason they did not become his own is that they were not willing. As a result, he is lamenting and weeping over their unwillingness to take hold of his call. Their assertion is strengthened as they note the verb "to will" is used twice, one expressing Jesus' will, and the other is attached to the people who rejected Jesus, thus presenting a paradigm of "I willed...but you were not willing." Pinson on this text states,

> "Jesus is willing for them to be under his wings, to be his own children. It is they who are unwilling. So there is nothing he can do about it, based on his plan of redemption for his free creatures. His weeping represents a true lament as Keener argues. Jesus love for Jerusalem here gives way to the brokenhearted pain of their rejection. The fact that they are not under his wings is to blame, not on his unwillingness, but on their unwillingness."[13]

The verse is used to argue against the Calvinist notion of irresistible grace by pointing out that Jesus was commanding the people to repent, and willed that they would do so, yet they did not do so because of their unwillingness.

Classical Arminians further point to examples where God calls individuals to respond to him in the Old Testament but they resist him and his persistent calls. It is asserted that God has done all he can to bring a people to himself by providing sufficient grace for mankind to respond. Often the example of the parable of the great banquet in Luke 14:16-24 is utilized to illustrate this point. The host has invited many individuals, yet that invitation has been refused. The invitation is a sincere and earnest invite into the great banquet, yet it can be resisted.

Arminianism and Irresistible Grace

Adding to what has been said thus far, we will now address Arminian responses to the Calvinist position of irresistible grace. A key text is found in John 6. Citing the relevant verses,

> "Jesus said to them, "I am the bread of life; whoever comes to me shall not hunger, and whoever believes in me shall never thirst. But I said to you that you have seen me and yet do not believe. All that the Father gives me will come to me, and whoever comes to me I will never cast out. For I have come down from heaven, not to do my own will but the will of him who sent me. And this is the will of him who sent me, that I should lose

The Doctrine of Grace

nothing of all that he has given me, but raise it up on the last day. For this is the will of my Father, that everyone who looks on the Son and believes in him should have eternal life, and I will raise him up on the last day."

So the Jews grumbled about him, because he said, "I am the bread that came down from heaven." They said, "Is not this Jesus, the son of Joseph, whose father and mother we know? How does he now say, 'I have come down from heaven'?" Jesus answered them, "Do not grumble among yourselves. No one can come to me unless the Father who sent me draws him. And I will raise him up on the last day. It is written in the Prophets, 'And they will all be taught by God.' Everyone who has heard and learned from the Father comes to me— not that anyone has seen the Father except he who is from God; he has seen the Father. Truly, truly, I say to you, whoever believes has eternal life. I am the bread of life. Your fathers ate the manna in the wilderness, and they died. This is the bread that comes down from heaven, so that one may eat of it and not die. I am the living bread that came down from heaven. If anyone eats of this bread, he will live forever. And the bread that I will give for the life of the world is my flesh."(John 6:35–51)

The Calvinist focuses on the statements that stress "all that the Father gives will go to the Son" in verses 37, 39, and 65. Also, the context of why the Jews did not believe, along with Jesus' apparent certainty that all that the Father gives 'will' come to him, proves 1) the reason the Jews do not believe is that they were neither drawn nor given to the Son and 2) the individuals who are drawn and given will certainly go to the Son. While the Calvinist explanation will be fleshed out below, the Arminian would contend that the passage does not argue for irresistible grace. Instead, the one who has believed is the one who has been given to Jesus by the Father. Regarding John 5:37-43, Pinson says,

> "Here Jesus tells his Jewish interlocutors that they have never heard the Father's voice and do not have his word abiding in them (vv. 37–38). Yet then he immediately tells them why they are in this condition: "because [hoti: since, because] you do not believe the one whom he sent" (v. 38, NRSV, NET), because "you refuse to come to me that you may have life" (v. 40), "you do not receive me" (v. 43, italics added). Thus the context of John 6:37 explains its meaning: Who is it that the Father gives Jesus? Those who do not refuse him (5:40), those who believe him (5:38), those who receive him (5:43). "He came to his own, and his own people did not receive him. But to all who did receive him, who believed in his name, he gave the right to become children of God" (John 1:11–12). It is clear that Jesus is holding out hope to these people that they can come to him if they stop refusing, if they believe him and receive him: "I say these things so that you may be saved" (6:34).[14]

The Arminian "believes that the sinner cannot come to Jesus unless the Father draws them (6:44), that the Father will give believers – those who do not refuse him – to his

Son, and that God must draw sinners and enable them with his grace for them to be saved. That is what John 6 is teaching, not irresistible grace."[15]

In summary, the Father gives those who believe in him to Jesus. Further, because of the text in John 12:32 where Jesus states that he will draw all people to himself, we find a universal granting and drawing in place where the condition of faith can be met in order to be 'given to the Son.' Pinson also stresses that individuals are drawn through divine teaching – God's gracious influence upon unbelievers with information about their lost state and the need for a savior.[16] John 6:45 comes into play here as Jesus states, "Everyone who has heard and learned from the Father comes to me." It is both hearing and learning of this divine teaching as well as not resisting this teaching that brings one to Jesus.

Conclusion on Arminianism and Grace

The Arminian believes the presentation of prevenient grace is crucial to the Arminian system as it allows them to reconcile or hold together the positions of total depravity, salvation by grace, human responsibility, and the offer of salvation to all. Calvinists agree with the importance of prevenient grace in the system of Arminianism, and will usually critique the system as a whole as lacking biblical support on the basis of prevenient grace which will be examined later. However, the Arminian asserts Calvinism fails because the call of God for people to obey and come to him is sometimes met with people's clear resistance to such grace. The Arminian says Calvinists leave God insincere in his general calling of all people when he only effectually calls some to respond positively.

Summarizing the position, Arminians believe there is a universal prevenient grace enabling and calling all men to receive the gift of faith and Christ, but this grace can be resisted. Man can choose whether to be one of the elect – those foreknown by God to have faith in Christ or the reprobate – those foreknown by God to resist God's grace.

Prevenient Grace in Classical Arminianism is not be confused with natural or general revelation. It is an individualized drawing that goes out to all people in God's own timing and manner. It is not a unilateral lessening of depravity but a working in an individual's heart and mind before conversion. Total depravity is not neutralized because of prevenient grace (as it sometimes is in Wesleyan Models). Furthermore, it is not the position that the atonement counteracts the effects of Adam's sin. Lastly, it is not that people can be saved without special revelation, the gospel, or confessing Christ.

Calvinism and Grace

As we move into the Calvinist understanding of grace, we first must note that Calvinists distinguish between common grace and special grace, similarly to the Arminian. The latter is our focus here, and we immediately come to points of divergence between the Calvinist and Arminian positions. As noted before, the Arminian position presents a universal prevenient grace that can be resisted, albeit in differently articulated forms. This is contrary to the Calvinist conception of a particular grace, that is, the grace only for those who are elect. This particular grace is irresistible. Irresistible grace makes up the I in TULIP. However, many Calvinists prefer to call this "effective," "efficacious," or even "invincible" grace because of misconceptions from the designation of "irresistible." Closely related to this is the notion of effectual calling. Because of its relevance, this section will examine the Calvinist distinction between the general call and the effectual call following our discussion on the effectual call.

Calvinism and Irresistible Grace

As with the Arminian position, grace is prevenient, as it goes before all Christ-honoring responses. However, the Calvinist understands this grace to be completely effectual because it will not fail to accomplish the task of bringing a people to God. The Calvinist tradition has noted that this calling and grace does not violate the human will but rather works in the man to change his will so that the man willingly comes to Christ. In some sense, effectual grace can be resisted, but only temporarily. This special grace is given to particular individuals chosen before the foundation of the world according to God's unconditional election, which is an election not based on the foreknown actions of a human's response to grace. Quoting the Westminster Confession of Faith, we read,

> "All those whom God hath predestinated unto life, and those only, he is pleased, in his appointed and accepted time, effectually to call, by his Word and Spirit, out of that state of sin and death in which they are by nature, to grace and salvation by Jesus Christ: enlightening their minds, spiritually and savingly, to understand the things of God, taking away their heart of stone, and giving unto them an heart of flesh; renewing their wills, and by his almighty power determining them to that which is good; and effectually drawing them to Jesus Christ; yet so as they come most freely, being made willing by his grace." (WCF 10.1)

This point is seen in the Canons of Dort as well, in the third and fourth head of doctrine article 11 where we read,

> "Moreover, when God carries out this good pleasure in his chosen ones, or works true conversion in them, he not only sees to it that the gospel is proclaimed to them outwardly, and enlightens their minds powerfully by the Holy Spirit so that they may rightly understand and discern the things of the Spirit of God, but, by the effective operation of the same regenerating Spirit, he also

penetrates into the inmost being of man, opens the closed heart, softens the hard heart, and circumcises the heart that is uncircumcised. He infuses new qualities into the will, making the dead will alive, the evil one good, the unwilling one willing, and the stubborn one compliant; he activates and strengthens the will so that, like a good tree, it may be enabled to produce the fruits of good deeds."

Article 16 continues to point out that,

"However, just as by the fall man did not cease to be man, endowed with intellect and will, and just as sin, which has spread through the whole human race, did not abolish the nature of the human race but distorted and spiritually killed it, so also this divine grace of regeneration does not act in people as if they were blocks and stones; nor does it abolish the will and its properties or coerce a reluctant will by force, but spiritually revives, heals, reforms, and – in a manner at once pleasing and powerful – bends it back. As a result, a ready and sincere obedience of the Spirit now begins to prevail where before the rebellion and resistance of the flesh were completely dominant. It is in this that the true and spiritual restoration and freedom of our will consists."

The Calvinist asserts that because God has determined to save a particular people, his determination will be accomplished. His will cannot be thwarted, nor will God be left to persuade and hope for the conversion of a particular people. However, this effectual working of God is not one of nullifying the human will, but rather changing the human will so man comes to God willingly. The misconception that God forces or coerces individuals to believe is a caricature of the Calvinistic position, likely created due to the strong language of Calvinists on the topic of God's compelling grace, which will be seen below.

Contrary to the assertion of the Arminian that this change of will is a violation or immoral, the Calvinist points out that God's intervention in the sinner's life to affect their will is not an act of immorality as some would make it, but a gracious and necessary intervention. He frees people to be as they were intended to be - creatures in right relationship with God. However, it needs to be remembered that this is not a grace given to everyone but only those who are the elect. It is an effectual calling.

Like the Arminians, Calvinists note texts such as John 6:44 and 65, which indicate that no man can go to Christ unless the Father draws or grants it to the individual. Further, Calvinists point out that "all that the Father" gives to Jesus "will" come to Christ. However, for the Calvinists, this text is not saying those who first believe are *then* given, and *then* 'will' come. Instead, the individuals will come *because* they are given. The statement that individuals 'will come' is the result of God's call.

Calvinists often point to the connection of the language of "drawing," to how it is used in various texts, such as Peter "drawing" out his sword in John 18:10 and Paul and Silas being "dragged" by a mob (Acts 16:19; 21:30). John 6:44 indicates to the Calvinist that the Father efficaciously calls the elect to Christ and that Christ says those who are called 'will' come, leaving little room for resistible grace. Another text on the point addresses the "Golden Chain of Redemption" found in Romans 8:30, which states, "And those whom he predestined he also called, and those whom he called he also justified and those whom he justified he also glorified." Shawn Wright says this verse teaches this effectual calling,

> "Starting in verse 29, Paul moves from foreknowledge to predestination to calling to justification to glorification. They are all intricately united, they are effective to accomplish their goal, and they result in the salvation of the elect. God's calling is as sure as his predestining."[17]

Because the calling is rooted in predestination and those whom God calls will be justified, the intended task of bringing people to Christ will be accomplished. All of this can further be clarified by understanding that Calvinists believe that God has two calls, a general call that is resistible, and an effectual call that is not. In this golden chain of redemption, those who have been called for God's good purpose cannot include everyone who has heard the gospel. The text assumes that those who are called receive this call positively.

Taking a position that leaves predestination up to God's foreknowledge of one's response makes this call incoherent. If God has predestined and called those whom he foreknew would respond positively, why is the salvific call universal rather than particular? The Arminian says this is necessary so that there is responsibility for rejecting the gospel. In contrast, the Calvinist believes that this responsibility stands regardless as the man is not choosing contrary to his nature. God has merely chosen not to extend mercy but enact judgment.

General vs. Effectual Calling

On the distinction between the general call and the effectual call, Wright says the following,

> "On the one hand, there is the general call (vocatio externa), which "refers to the call to all people to pay heed to the revelation of God." Anthony Hoekema defines it this way: "The offering of salvation in Christ to people, together with an invitation to accept Christ in repentance and faith, in order that they may receive the forgiveness of sins and eternal life." This general, outward call of God occurs through creation and conscience, summoning people to "acknowledge and honor their Creator (Ps. 19:1–4; Acts 17:24; Rom. 1:19–21; 2:14–15)." But it also occurs through God's verbal summons to sinners to "repentance and faith in Christ so that they may receive eternal life and be forgiven of their trespasses (Matt. 28:18–20; Acts 1:6–8; 26:16–23; Rom. 10:8–15; 1 Cor. 15:1–8)." This general, outward call goes to all persons. It's a real summons to submit to God. When the gospel is extended, it includes the offer of salvation. Yet people resist it all the time, because "the gospel call goes to all people but it is clearly not intended to be effectual for all of them, for we know that not all do in fact believe."[18]

The general call is noted in the Calvinistic confessions as well,

> "Others not-elected, although they may be called by the ministry of the word, and may have some common operations of the Spirit, yet not being effectually drawn by the Father, they neither will, nor can truly come to Christ; and therefore cannot be saved: much less can men that receive not the Christian religion be saved; be they never so diligent to frame their lives according to the light of nature, and the Law of that religion they do profess."[19]

The confessions point out that individuals who may be under the preaching of the gospel and hear it are "called by the ministry of the word yet are not effectually drawn by the Spirit." Further, it notes that they may have some common operations of the Spirit (citing Hebrews 6:4-5), like some sharing in doctrine, intellectual understanding of the faith, and Christian life amid a body of believers, yet have not been effectually called and are unregenerate. Bruce Demarest points to the wedding banquet parable to demonstrate this dynamic (Matthew 22:1-14; Luke 14:16-24).[20] Demarest argues that the parable distinguishes between God's universal general call and his particular effectual call. The first group in the parable resisted the call as they were more concerned with worldly interests and felt indifferent. The invitees rejected the invitation and were punished. Demarest continues,

"Consequently, the king sent his servants to bring to the banquet the unfit and unworthy, an act that signifies the successful preaching of Jesus and his apostles to outcast Jews and Gentiles. The latter invitations accomplished the intended purpose, in that a crowd of people joined the king for the wedding feast."[21]

Demarest goes on to say that the second and third calls to the feast involve the language of "bringing in" guests and "make them come in" while the first group did not have this compelling movement. The parable ends with Jesus' words, "For many are called, but few are chosen." Demarest states, "The called represents the larger group summoned by invitation. The chosen were the smaller group forcefully brought to the banquet."[22]

Contrary to this resistible general call, God sovereignly calls some to faith in Christ, and this invitation is internal, wherein God's drawing people to Christ is always effective in accomplishing its goal. The Calvinist argument is connected to God's purposes and the accomplishing of his will. God does not fail in his will to save those whom he predestined. This means that foreknowledge and predestination are necessary components to fully appreciate the Calvinist's contention with resistible grace. Still, Calvinists critique the Arminian conception that God has and is trying his best to bring people to him but failing when his salvific call is resisted.

Because irresistible grace is closely linked with God's purposes and plans in the Calvinist position, other texts are evoked, such as John 10 where Jesus speaks of being the good shepherd who knows his sheep. The text, which will also be brought to the forefront when discussing the atonement in Calvinism, notes the following:

- The shepherd of the sheep enters by the gate (v. 2)
- The sheep hear his voice (v. 3)
- The shepherd calls his own sheep by name and leads them out (v. 3)
- The Shepherd goes before them, and the sheep follow and know his voice (v. 4)
- Jesus is the Shepherd "who knows his own and my own know me" (v. 14)
- Jesus explains he has other sheep to "bring" and they "will listen to my voice." (v. 16)
- Jesus explains that the unbelievers "do not believe because you are not among my sheep" (v. 26)
- "My sheep hear my voice, and I know them, and they follow me" (v. 27)
- "I give them eternal life, and they will never perish" (v. 28)
- "No one will snatch them out of my hand" (v. 28)

The Calvinist points out firstly how God's plan is expressed in the coming of the shepherd, the calling and gathering of the sheep, the preservation of the sheep, and the explanation of unbelievers to Jesus' contemporaries.

First, we read that the sheep hear and recognize the shepherd's voice who calls the sheep by name and leads them. The sheep then follow the shepherd as they know his voice. The shepherd knows each sheep, and they know him. Next, when speaking to the unbelievers, he explains their unbelief as the result of them not being "among his sheep." Finally, Jesus says that the sheep will not perish. In fact, they will never perish and cannot be snatched from his hand as the protective shepherd.

The calling and the knowledge between Jesus and the sheep becomes a critical point for the Calvinists on the effectual call. This, in conjunction with texts such as 2 Timothy 2:19 where Paul states that "The Lord knows who are his," and the saints are designated as 'those whom are called' become a basis for irresistible grace. While we have not been comprehensive with the texts that are utilized for the Calvinist's position, we will move into Calvinism's response to resistible grace.

The General vs. Effectual Call in Calvinism

Calvinism and Resistible Grace

When addressing resistible grace, Calvinists generally find no issue with the typical texts cited wherein man has resisted God and his call. As noted prior, Calvinists distinguish between the general and effectual calls, the former of which can be resisted. Further, in dialogues between Calvinists and Classical Arminians, Calvinist objections to resistible grace often focus upon a rejection of the universal prevenient grace as presented by Arminians.

This is because prevenient grace acts as an essential counter to irresistible grace. Because both Arminians and Calvinists agree that man is depraved and needs grace in order to respond to God, and because the effectual calling is similar to prevenient grace in some sense, discussions center around the extent of this effectual calling. Is it only bestowed upon the elect? Or is it for everyone?

The Arminian's position of prevenient grace allows them to affirm total depravity, and yet that grace aids all people so that they can respond to the gospel. It makes people savable by bringing people into a place where they are moved from being unable to respond to being able to respond. Prevenient grace allows for libertarian freedom of the will and total depravity to exist in harmony. Calvinists have rejected this understanding of prevenient grace because of a lack of scriptural support.

While some texts are used to infer prevenient grace, Calvinists argue that none work in favor of the position when scrutinized. The Arminian typically points to texts they believe necessitate the concept of universal prevenient grace. These scriptures speak about God commanding and desiring all people to repent like Acts 17:20 and 2 Peter 3:9. Their reasoning is that these texts indicate or presuppose the ability to respond to the gospel has been given to people. Other texts will also be evoked such as John Wesley's favored text of John 1:9 and the often-cited John 12:32 wherein the gospel says that Christ will "draw all men to himself."

The Calvinist believes these texts fail to make a case for the Arminian conception of universal prevenient grace. For example, John Wesley's often cited John 1:9,

"The true light, which gives light to everyone, was coming into the world," does not amount to an inward work of illumination and enablement. Instead, this is describing the general illumination of Christ's coming into the world, likened to exposure from a light. This is seen in the context of John in v. 10-11, which demonstrates that this light is not a means of enablement but exposure as "some are shown to be evil because they did not know or receive Jesus."[23] Thomas Schreiner points out that evil men shrink from the light because they do not want to be exposed in verse 20, and those who practice truth come to the light in verse 21. "The light exposes and reveals the moral and spiritual state of one's heart...it shows where people are in their relationship to God,"[24] John 1:9 does not advocate for a universal prevenient grace. What of John 12:32, which reads, "And I, when I am lifted up from the earth, will draw all people to myself"? Calvinists point out that it is the less likely option to suggest that this "all" refers to every individual but rather, in conjunction with texts such as 10:16 and 11:52, it refers to every *type* of person, namely Gentiles, and Jews.[25] Michaels states,

> "Another recourse is to understand "all" (whether read as masculine or neuter) in relation to ethnic groups rather than individuals. That is, both Jews and Greeks.[57] This could be supported by an appeal to Paul (especially in Romans), for whom "all" frequently comes to mean "Jew and Greek" (or "Jew and Gentile") alike (see, for example, Rom 1:18; 2:9, 10; 3:9, 23; 10:12; 11:32). It can also appeal, obviously, to the actual presence of

"Greeks" in the narrative context (vv. 20–22). This option has much in its favor, and many modern interpreters have adopted it."[26]

Michaels also points out,

> "The verb "I will draw" is in fact the likely key to the meaning of the verse. Those "drawn" are a specific group, those who actually "come" to Jesus in faith, for salvation. The repeated expression, "to come to me" (6:37, 44, and 65), corresponds to the promise here that Jesus will draw these people "to myself," suggesting that the same specific group is in mind here. If so, then "all" is qualified by the previous references to those "drawn" or "given" to Jesus by the Father, that is, believers (hence the translation, "them all"). The point is not that every human being is "drawn," but that all those drawn by the Father are drawn by the Son. Instead of the Father drawing believers to Jesus, he himself, now "lifted up from the earth," draws "them all" to himself. As he put it in the earlier setting, "I will raise him up at the last day" (6:44). Jesus will "draw" believers first to the cross on which he is "lifted up" (see v. 33), but beyond that to wherever he is going (see v. 26, "where I am, there my servant will be")."[27]

The Calvinists find no scriptural warrant for prevenient grace on the basis of vital Arminian texts. Before moving on to the questions raised from texts such as Acts 17:20 and 2 Peter 3:9 and God's will, we will note a few more critiques of prevenient grace that Calvinists present.

According to the Calvinist, the Arminian notion gives man something he can boast about. Every man receives grace, but it is only the one who made a good and wise choice to follow Christ who will be saved. That person, for whatever reason, embraced the gift of faith and was better, smarter, and deserving of credit for heeding the call. Calvinists further critique that the Arminian position has election based on those who will have faith, yet faith is a gift of God (Eph. 2:8-10; Phil. 1:29; 2 Pet. 1:1; 2 Tim. 2:24-26; Acts 5:31; 11:18). Sam Storms summarizes another critique as follows:

> "The Arminian contends that God foreknows both that some are and others are not going to believe in Christ in response to the gospel. He also affirms that God knows why they respond either in belief or unbelief, for God is omniscient and knows the secrets and inner motives of the heart. God also knows what it is in the presentation of the gospel that proves successful in persuading some to say "Yes" and what it is that proves unsuccessful in persuading those who say "No." The question, then, is this: If God truly desires for all to be saved in the way the Arminian contends, and if he knows what it is in the means of persuasion contained in the gospel that brings people to say yes, why doesn't he orchestrate the presentation of the gospel in such a way that it will succeed in persuading all people to believe? The point is this: Surely the God who perfectly knows every human heart is capable of creating a world in which the gospel would prove successful in every case. And if God desires for

all to be saved in the way that Arminian contends, why didn't he?[28]

From the Calvinist perspective, the Arminian model has God simply doing the best he can to save people and is failing to do so, with his will and desires thwarted by the will of men. Calvinists point out that in Calvinism, God has chosen to show mercy to people and succeeds in executing his will to redeem a particular people. While Arminians sometimes critique Calvinism by suggesting there are a 'few' who are elect, though the 'few' is a strawman, the Calvinist responds that in the Arminian schema, there is no limit to how low the number of saved could be. This number can lower even more for Arminians who believe that a Christian can lose their salvation.

The Two Wills of God

The discussion of 2 Peter 3:9 and how Calvinists understand this text helps inform the overall framework. How texts like this are understood in Calvinism relate closely to God's two wills. Before going further than this, it is worth prefacing this section by pointing out that the critique often levied at Calvinists, that the "two wills of God" concept is a construct to work around complex texts, is unfair. The critique is unfair, as Arminians also have a twofold understanding of God's will and apply it to libertarian freedom of the will (see Chapter 3).

With this in mind we can now discuss the will of God, how it is understood in a twofold sense in Calvinism, and what the biblical basis is for such a position. For this discussion, we'll be relying on the explanation by Shawn Wright, who begins his description as follows,

> "The Bible teaches us that from our perspective God's will (which is always one) would be understood in a twofold sense. First is his revealed-to-us (in Scripture) will; second is his hidden from us, known only to himself secret will. This twofold understanding leads to the conclusion that there are two wills in God regarding human salvation. At the same time that he desires the salvation of all persons, our Lord determines to save only his chosen ones."[29]

Within the Calvinist framework, God is not influenced in different directions as we are. Instead, God has all the power to do whatever he desires, and "God's will has no causes outside his wise decision that something should occur."[30] Further, Wright states, "God's will, then, is one, for his will takes place according to his decree, his determination, his counsel, his purpose"[31] while pointing to Ephesians 1:5; 11, Isaiah 46:10, Psalm 115:3, and Psalm 135:6. This reality with the seemingly conflicting picture of man and devils disobeying God's will leads to an understanding that there is a distinction to be made between the secret will of God and the revealed will of God. This is described as follows,

> "On the one hand, God has an eternally planned will (decreed or secret because it has been ordained from eternity and is known perfectly only unto him) which will surely come to pass. It is God's decree, 'his eternal

purpose, by which he foreordaines everything that comes to pass.' On the other hand, God has a will in which he tells us what he desires for us to do. This is why it is also called his revealed or preceptive will, since it has been made known to us and comes to us in the form of commands or expectations of how we should live before God; but he does not sovereignty decree that we shall do this will. Frame concludes that, 'God's decretive will cannot be successfully opposed; it will certainly take place. It is possible, however, and often the case, for creatures to disobey God's preceptive will."[32]

Wright explains that this distinction protects God's integrity as well as human responsibility and then quotes Dabney for explanation,

"Every man is impelled to make the distinction; for otherwise, either alternative is odious and absurd. Say that God has no secret decretive will, and he wishes just what he commands and nothing more, and we represent him as a being whose desires are perpetually crossed and baffled: yea, trampled on; the most harassed, embarrassed, and impotent being in the universe. Deny the other part of our distinction, and you represent God as acquiescing in all the inequities done on earth and in hell."[33]

Regarding scripture, Wright points out that in various texts, we find that God "means" for a particular result even when man is disobedient such as in Genesis 50:20. A

The Doctrine of Grace

case study is found in the events of Pharaoh's hardened heart and the exodus. God's will is that Pharaoh let the Israelites go, yet the Lord also tells Moses that *he* will harden Pharaoh's heart so that "he will not let my people go." Wright states, "We must surmise, then, that there is 'the will of command (let my people go) and the will of decree (God hardened Pharaoh's heart)."[34]

When this applies to salvation, Wright looks to Luke 13:34 and Matthew 11:25-26. The former text reads,

> "O Jerusalem, Jerusalem, the city that kills the prophets and stones those who are sent to it! How often *would I have gathered* your children together as a hen gathers her brood under her wings, and you would not! (Luke 13:34; italics added).

The latter reads,

> "I thank you, Father, Lord of heaven and earth, that you have hidden these things from the wise and understanding and revealed them to little children; yes, Father, *for such was your gracious will.* All things have been handed over to me by my Father, and no one knows the Father except the Son and anyone to whom the Son chooses to reveal him." (Matt. 11:25–27; italics added).

Wright points out these are seemingly contradictory declarations and states, "the conclusion we come to, then, is that Jesus in some sense really willed both of these things. He really desired all in Jerusalem to be saved. At the same time, he willed that only certain people in Israel would be saved."[35]

> "Every man is impelled to make the distinction; for otherwise, either alternative is odious and absurd. Say that God has no secret decretive will, and he wishes just what he commands and nothing more, and we represent him as a being whose desires are perpetually crossed and baffled: yea, trampled on; the most harassed, embarrassed, and impotent being in the universe. Deny the other part of our distinction, and you represent God as acquiescing in all the inequities done on earth and in hell."[36]

This moves us into how Calvinists understand texts such as 2 Peter 3:9 and 1 Timothy 2:3-4. While there can be a critique of the Calvinist for the tension, such a tension is also found within Arminianism with differing beginning and ending points. Wright summarizes helpfully again,

> "Both Arminians and Calvinists admit that there are (from our perspective) these two sorts of wills in God (as long as they remember at the same time that God's will is one and simple). But evangelical Arminians do not believe God's desire for the salvation of all persons will lead to universalism. Rather, they reason something like this: "What does God will more than saving all? The answer given by Arminians is that human self-determination and the possible resulting love relationship with God are more valuable than saving people by sovereign, efficacious grace." In this scheme, God's will to let

humans (aided by prevenient grace) make their libertarian choice for Jesus takes priority over his will to save people. Calvinism is different. For Calvinists, according to Piper, "the greater value is the manifestation of the full range of God's glory in wrath and mercy (Rom. 9:22–23) and the humbling of man so that he enjoys giving all credit to God for his salvation (1 Cor. 1:29)." Arminians emphasize the priority of libertarian human freedom. Calvinists emphasize the priority of divine sovereign freedom. Piper is correct: Since not all people are saved we must choose whether we believe (with the Arminians) that God's will to save all people is restrained by his commitment to human self-determination or whether we believe (with the Calvinists) that God's will to save all people is restrained by his commitment to the glorification of his sovereign grace. (Eph. 1:6, 12, 14; Rom. 9.22–23)"[37]

Conclusion on Calvinism and Grace

Unlike Arminianism, grace is irresistible and particular in Calvinism. The special work of God's grace only goes out to those who God has effectually called, and those who are called are likewise justified and finally glorified because God will not fail to bring a people to himself. While a man who is effectually called can resist for a time, he will ultimately come to faith willingly, not against his will. Furthermore, while God's effectual calling is irresistible, the general call of God is resistible and indeed is often willfully-resisted.

Summary

The Calvinist viewpoint holds that grace is irresistible and particular, reserved for those divinely and effectually called. These individuals, though they may resist for a while, ultimately embrace faith willingly. In contrast, the general call of God can be, and often is, willfully resisted. Meanwhile, Arminianism posits the concept of a universal prevenient grace, which extends the potential for faith to all but allows for its rejection. The Arminian conception of grace generally is not a neutralization of depravity nor is it an impersonal force.

Chapter 5
Conversion and Regeneration

We will now briefly discuss conversion and regeneration in the Arminian and Calvinist frameworks. While Calvinists and Arminians both hold that faith is a gift from God via texts such as Philippians 1:29 and Ephesians 2:8-10, our discussion is necessary because Calvinists and Arminians generally disagree on what is called the ordo salutis, or the order of salvation. The divergences between the two views are simple enough to consider in brief before moving into the doctrine of election.

Overall, the disagreement between Arminianism and Calvinism is on whether regeneration (being born again) comes before or after faith. Within Calvinism, most have historically held that regeneration precedes faith, although some, such as Millard Erickson and Bruce Demarest, hold that faith comes first. For example, Bruce Demarest in The Cross and Salvation explains that,

"Most scriptures represent saving faith as a condition of God's regenerating work. The notion that God regenerates prior to the sinner's response of penitent faith (chronologically or logically) appears to be Biblically unwarranted. The spiritual dynamic that prompts and empowers sinners to convert resides not in regeneration but in the power of the Spirit's effectual calling."[1]

Erickson echoes this position, which isn't limited to the two of them, but can be seen in some earlier Calvinists as well. Furthermore, most discussions on the order of salvation focus on a logical rather than a chronological order. This means that generally theologians will focus on the logical connections between the different aspects of salvation rather than trying to create a timeline of events. However, some stress the chronological aspects to the point where regeneration can occur a significant amount of time before faith.

Most Calvinists believe that regeneration preceding faith is one of the key distinctions between Calvinism and Arminianism. In Calvinist circles, R.C. Sproul seems to have popularized the emphasis upon this distinction as he called this "a cardinal doctrine of Reformed theology."[2] Shawn Wright, when describing the issue, says the following,

"Calvinists' views are significantly different from Arminians'. Holding to prevenient grace, Arminians deny that God chooses to be gracious to a particular set of individuals. Rather, based on his foreknowledge of who will respond to the gospel, God chooses those future responders. When they repent and believe of their own free will, they are born again. In other words, in Arminianism faith precedes regeneration. Believing in Christ causes one to be born again. For this reason, Arminians are synergists. They maintain that sinners cooperate with God in the process of salvation. Calvinists believe that because of the utter sinfulness, and resulting spiritual inability, of humanity, regeneration must precede faith. One is born from above, born by the power of the Holy Spirit (John 3:5–8) and then, as a result, the person believes in Jesus. For this reason, Calvinists are monergists, that is, those who hold that God is the sole cause of salvation since sinners are mired in sin. Monergism comports with the Bible's teaching on sin, God's efficacious grace, and the relationship between regeneration and faith."[3]

Here, one can see that the Calvinist position is concerned about maintaining monergism and that it is God's work from beginning to end in bringing a people to salvation. The Calvinist also asserts that if man is enabled to believe the gospel in a grace that comes before, he will still choose sin if he is not given a new heart and inclination towards God. For many Calvinists, placing faith before regeneration is a compromise of total depravity or a door to giving credit to the man who takes hold of faith, allowing him to boast. Furthermore, faith coming before regeneration logically entails cooperating with grace and effecting one's regeneration. It is argued that even in passive acceptance of faith, it is a movement of the will to not reject grace which the Calvinist seeks to avoid.

Texts that are used to support this are found in verses describing the corruption of man, particularly 1 John 5:1. The text reads that "Everyone who believes that Jesus is the Christ has been born of God, and everyone who loves the Father loves whoever has been born of him." The argument is that those who have believed have already been born again. Without going into the grammatical argument, Thomas Schreiner's summary is helpful,

> "No evangelical would say that before we are born again we must practice righteousness, for such a view would teach works-righteousness. Nor would we say that first we avoid sinning, and then are born of God, for such a view would suggest that human works cause us to be born of God. Nor would we say that first we show great love for God, and then he causes us to be born again. No, it is clear that practicing righteousness, avoiding sin, and loving are all the consequences or results of the new birth. But if this is the case, then we must interpret 1 John 5:1 in the same way, for the structure of the verse is the same as what we find in the texts about practicing righteousness (1 John 2:29), avoiding sin (1 John 3:9), and loving God (1 John 4:7). It follows, then, that 1 John 5:1 teaches that first God grants us new life and then we believe Jesus is the Christ."[4]

The bottom line and concern for this particular distinction is that regeneration is a work of God and not dependent upon a human response or human activity. As mentioned above, the issue is of logical order rather than chronological order, recognizing that placing regeneration before faith chronologically, even by seconds, would mean that there is a 'new creature in Christ' who is not a believer. Matt Slick points out, by flipping the paradigm, that the issue remains for those who place chronological strain on faith coming before regeneration, "if faith precedes regeneration, let's say by five seconds, then we would have someone who is a believer but is also not regenerate for about five seconds. See the problem?"[5] Slick's overall summary is helpful,

> "Arminians assert that we must believe in order to become Christians and when we become Christians we are regenerated. Calvinists assert that a person is not able to believe of his own free will because of the doctrine of total depravity (that his free will is a slave of sin). Therefore, in the Calvinist camp regeneration precedes faith. Each side is with its proponents and opponents as well as strengths and weaknesses. However, since I lean towards the Calvinist camp, I hold to regeneration preceding faith. But not in a temporal sense. Let me explain with an illustration. In a light bulb, electricity must be in place in order for light to occur. But, it is not true that light must be in place for electricity to occur. The light is dependent on the electricity, not the other way around. Therefore, the electricity is logically first, but not temporally first because when the electricity is present, light is the necessary and simultaneous result. Likewise, regeneration must be in place in order for believing to occur. When regeneration is in place, faith is the necessary and simultaneous result. Finally, when we say logical order we must

clarify that it is not an order of temporality, but of logical necessity."[6]

Arminians typically critique the notion that regeneration precedes faith with the chronological presentation in mind. How can one have spiritual life without faith and thus apart from Christ? It is further critiqued that this is placing sanctification before justification, as Calvinists have generally stated, "regeneration is the beginning of sanctification."[7] Forlines says the following on the point,

> "God cannot perform the act of regeneration (an act of sanctification) in a person before he or she is justified. God can move in with His sanctifying grace only after the guilt problem is satisfied by justification. To think otherwise is to violate the law of non-contradiction. I realize that when we talk about the ordo salutis (order of salvation) we are talking about logical order instead of chronological order. But that logical order is inviolable!"[8]

Arminianism further points out that in the New Testament, the whole of salvation is by faith, but particularly being children of God and being born again. For texts such as John 1:12-13, where the Calvinist stresses that this being born again is "not by the will of man," the Arminian emphasizes that the condition of being made children of God is 'receiving him,' placing faith prior logically.

Summary

As mentioned prior, not all Calvinists today hold to regeneration preceding faith. Still, most do, as it has been stressed as an axiom of the Calvinist tradition by teachers such as R.C. Sproul. On the point of conversion, Calvinists and Arminians both hold that faith is a gift for man to take hold of. Classical Arminians hold in agreement with Calvinists that justification is by faith. The disagreements can be summarized in whether special grace is particular or universal, whether grace is resistible or irresistible, and typically whether regeneration precedes or follows faith.

Order of Salvation In Calvinism:

- Unconditional Election
- Calling
- Regeneration
- Faith
- Justification
- Sanctification
- Glorification

Order of Salvation In Arminianism:

- Conditional Election
- Prevenient Grace
- Faith
- Justification
- Regeneration
- Sanctification
- Glorification

Chapter 6
Predestination and Election

As we move into the waters of predestination and election, it would be impossible to address every aspect of this topic. Instead, we will look at critical issues and texts while summarizing how Calvinists and Arminians reason through them. When examining unconditional and conditional election, we'll revisit the issue of foreknowledge, which was briefly discussed in the chapter on the human will. Circling back to this topic of foreknowledge will be unavoidable because it plays a role in the question of whether election is conditional or unconditional. First, we will define election and describe predestination, then move into the Arminian presentation on the subject.

What is Election?

Beginning with a simple definition from the Pocket Theological Terms, we read that election is,

> "A biblical word used to speak of God's choosing of individuals or people to bring about God's good purposes. In general terms *election* can refer to God's choosing of persons for a type of service, while in a more particular sense *election* refers to God's choosing of persons to inherit salvation through Jesus Christ. The doctrine of election has been the subject of intense debate, particularly between Calvinist and Arminian theologians, since the Reformation era. Other theologians (e.g., Karl Barth) try to avoid the Calvinist-Arminian debate by suggesting that God's election is first and foremost an election of Christ rather than the election of individuals to salvation."[1]

The Holman Bible Dictionary defines election as,

> "God's plan to bring salvation to His people and His world. The doctrine of election is at once one of the most central and one of the most misunderstood teachings of the Bible. At its most basic level, election refers to the purpose or plan of God whereby He has determined to effect His will. Thus election encompasses the entire range of divine activity from creation, God's decision to bring the world into being out of nothing, to the end time, the making anew of heaven and earth. The word "election" itself is derived from the Greek word, *ekle-*

gomai, which means, literally, "to choose something for oneself." This in turn corresponds to the Hebrew word, *bachar*. The objects of divine selection are the elect ones, a concept found with increasing frequency in the later writings of the OT and at many places in the NT (Matt. 22:14; Luke 18:7; Col. 3:12; Rev. 17:14). The Bible also uses other words such as "choose," "predestinate," "foreordain," "determine," and "call" to indicate that God has entered into a special relationship with certain individuals and groups through whom He has decided to fulfill His purpose within the history of salvation."[2]

The Holman Bible dictionary helpfully points out five significant Old Testament motifs concerning the election of Israel. Firstly, that election results from God's initiative (cf. Abraham as an example, Genesis 12:1-7). Secondly, the word in Israel's vocabulary for their relationship to God is "covenant," a bond established by God's unmerited grace (Deuteronomy 7:6-7). Thirdly, within the covenant community, God selected particular individuals for particular tasks or functions, such as Aaron, Moses, David, etc. Fourth, Israel's election was an opportunity for service to God, not a pretext for pride. Finally, in the later Old Testament writings and during the intertestamental period, the elect ones are considered the true and faithful remnant amid the people of God.[3]

To quote George in his contribution on election in the New Testament,

"Early Christians saw themselves as heirs of Israel's election, "a chosen race, a royal priesthood, a holy nation, a people for His possession" (1 Pet. 2:9 HCSB). Paul treats this theme most extensively, but we should not overlook its central importance for the entire NT. Again, certain individuals are singled out as chosen by God: the 12 apostles (Luke 6:13), Peter (Acts 15:7), Paul (Acts 9:15), and Jesus Himself (Luke 9:35; 23:35). In the Synoptic gospels the term "elect ones" is always set in an eschatological context, that is, the days of tribulation will be shortened "because of the elect, whom He chose" (Mark 13:20 HCSB). Many of the parables of Jesus, such as that of the marriage feast (Matt. 22:1-14) and that of the laborers in the vineyard (Matt. 20:1-16), illustrate the sovereignty of God in salvation. In John, Jesus is the unmistakable Mediator of election: "You did not choose Me, but I chose you," He reminded the disciples (John 15:16a HCSB). Again, His followers are those who have been given to Him by the Father "before the world existed" and "not one of them is lost" (John 17:5,12 HCSB). Also in John the shadow side of election is posed in the person of Judas, "the son of destruction." Though his status as one of the elect is called into question by his betrayal of Christ, not even this act was able to thwart the fulfillment of God's plan of salvation.[4]

When speaking to election as it is seen in Paul's literature, George states,

> There are three passages where Paul deals at length with different aspects of the doctrine of election. In the first (Rom. 8:28-39) divine election is presented as the ground and assurance of the Christian's hope. Since

those whom God has predestinated are also called, justified, and glorified, nothing can separate them from the love of God in Christ Jesus. The second passage (Rom. 9–11) is preoccupied with the fact of Israel's rejection of Christ which, in the purpose of God, has become the occasion for the entrance of Gentile believers into the covenant. In the third passage (Eph. 1:1-12) Paul pointed to the Christocentric character of election: God has chosen us "in Christ" before the foundation of the world. We can refer to this statement as the evangelical center of the doctrine of election. Our election is strictly and solely in Christ. As the eternal Son, He is along with the Father and the Holy Spirit, the electing God; as the incarnate Mediator between God and humankind, He is the elected One. We should never speak of predestination apart from this central truth."[5]

What is Predestination?

Though predestination and election are closely tied together, a definition of the former may be helpful before proceeding. Chad Brand summarizes it as

> "God's purposes in grace directed towards those whom he will ultimately save to the uttermost. The word predestine as a verb with God as its subject is used six times in the NT (Acts 4:28; Romans 8:29: 1 Corinthians 2:7; Ephesians 1:5;11). The word...means essentially, "to decide upon beforehand." Other words convey a similar idea: to determine, to elect, to foreknow."[6]

Essentially, predestination deals with God's sovereign determination. In regards to salvation specifically, predestination is choosing beforehand, before the creation of the world, who will be saved. To avoid bias in my articulation, I will pause there.

At this point, several questions begin to form: does God elect or choose people to service only, to salvation, or to both? And is election conditional upon one's response to the gospel or unconditional in that God chooses according to his will? Additionally, is election corporate, individual, or both, meaning does God elect the class of people or does he select people individually? Further, does God elect people both unto salvation and damnation? Each respective position will answer these questions.

Election and Predestination in Arminianism

We will begin answering the aforementioned questions by merging the first two because of the general agreement between Calvinists and Arminians. We will then answer the remaining questions from the Arminian perspective. The first question is, "Does God elect or choose people to service only, to salvation, or to both?" the second is, "Is election corporate, individual, or both, meaning does God elect the class of people, whether in Christ or in Adam or does he elect people individually?"

Classical Arminians and Calvinists find agreement that God elects people to salvation and also for service. Those elected to salvation are, by extension, called to service. Furthermore, both Calvinists and Arminians typically agree that there is both a corporate and individual aspect to election. Matthew Pinson on the Arminian conception of election and predestination states,

> "The classic Arminian doctrine of predestination, however, is that God does indeed choose individuals. He elects believers for eternal salvation and reprobates unbelievers to eternal damnation. Hence the traditional Arminian doctrine is the conditional election of individuals."[7]

Roger Olson also affirms the conditional election of individuals to salvation while stating that the election of the church is unconditional.[8] Olson explains that in Arminianism, there is both a conditional and unconditional election. He says, "Arminians do not believe God predetermines or preselects people for either heaven or hell apart from their free acts of accepting or resisting the grace of God."[9] The election of the individual to salvation is conditional upon that individual's acceptance of the grace of God, hence, conditional election. Yet,

> "Arminians interpret the biblical concept of unconditional election (predestination to salvation) as corporate. Thus, predestination has an individual meaning (foreknowledge of individual choices) and a collective meaning (election of a people). The former is conditional; the latter is unconditional. God's predestination of individuals is conditioned by their faith; God's election of a people for his glory is unconditional. The latter will comprise all those who believe."[10]

Arminian Grant Osborne and Matthew Pinson assert that the modern Arminian emphasis on corporate election, at the expense of individual election, is a newer development that makes distinctions with little difference in that

> "God has chosen individuals who form the church. Cottrell argues, among other things, that one biblical image of individual election is the elect's very names being written in the book of life: "What can this be but individual predestination?"[11]

This finds agreement with Calvinists in that the modern shift in focus to corporate election at the expense of individual election is a false dichotomy because individuals always make up a corporate body. This point of agreement between Calvinists and Classical Arminians is worth noting. Pinson, along with Olson and others, argues that the classical position in Arminianism has always maintained individual and corporate election together.[12] Pinson goes on to state,

> "Almost no orthodox Christian from before the seventeenth century affirmed what is today called corporate election. An examination of Arminius gets us back in touch with this tradition of Christian teaching... Arminius discussed only individuals in connection with the New Testament doctrine of predestination and election. Of course, he discussed individuals in both the singular and the plural. This is necessary to say, because some theologians who advocate corporate election use the New Testament's plural language as evidence of corporate election, as though when Paul says in Ephesians 1:5 "having predestined us to adoption as sons by Jesus Christ to Himself, according to the good pleasure of His will," this entails corporate election because the language is plural. However, this is a flawed premise, since it would entail that I, as an individual Christian, have not been adopted as a son.
>
> Arminius's writings on election are permeated with individual language. He believed that God is always relating to people in his predestining decrees, whether elective or reprobative, as individual persons. Thus, for example, he averred that, though Christ died for the reprobate, he did not "hold" them "as his own," and "them He does not know as His own, or acknowledge

as His own," but he did acknowledge the elect as his own."[13]

Pinson points out that Classical Arminianism does not create an abstract election of classes as corporate election is forced to, but rather that election is conditional along with reprobation being conditional and individual.

The Arminian position argues for conditional election on the basis that salvation is conditioned in believing and election is conditioned on belief. Pinson states,

> "predestination is an eternal administration of what is taking place in the lives of the elect in time. Thus, if salvation and damnation are conditional, then election and reprobation are conditional. This accords with the gospel revealed in Holy Scripture."[14]

To be elect and predestined to salvation in conditional election is to be foreknown by God to have accepted his gift of faith. To be rebrobate (predestined to damnation) is to be foreknown by God to have rejected his gift of faith. This predestination and election occurred before the foundation of the world based on God's simple foreknowledge. God knew who would choose him and who would not (see chapter 3, Arminianism and Foreknowledge). To put it another way, to be the elect and predestined to salvation is to meet the condition of accepting faith, hence "conditional election." To be damned is to meet the condition of rejecting the gift. Arminians articulate this as conditional double predestination.

Because of the agreement between Calvinists and

Arminians regarding individual election to salvation, the question ultimately becomes whether or not key texts teach unconditional or conditional election. The former being based on nothing seen in man – specifically foreknown faith or acceptance of the gospel, but wholly on God's will, and the latter being based on those who will accept the call of the gospel. Next, we will look at how Arminians reason through some key texts, relying on Pinson and Forlines to guide us.

Romans 8:28-30 and Arminianism

A key text reads,

> "And we know that for those who love God all things work together for good, for those who are called according to his purpose. For those whom he foreknew he also predestined to be conformed to the image of his Son, in order that he might be the firstborn among many brothers. And those whom he predestined he also called, and those whom he called he also justified, and those whom he justified he also glorified." (Romans 8:28–30)

The question of this text centers around whether "foreknew" refers to what God knows to be true in the future (he knows who will have faith) or if God foreknew in such a way because he predestined. Put another way, does the verb translated as "foreknew" in this verse indicate prescience (foresight) or foreordination (ordaining something to come to pass beforehand)?

Pinson and Forlines argue that "to know beforehand" is how the term should be understood and push back against the notion of the term carrying "foreordination" in it because each of the terms used in Romans 8:28-30 build upon one another and are not synonymous. In other words, foreordination would be redundant next to predestination when the text indicates foreknowledge leads to predestination.[15] Furthermore, Pinson and Jacob Arminius find agreement with Calvinists in that the term "foreknowledge" denotes this idea of foreloving a people, but they say this is not only an affectionate knowledge but also the foresight of those believer's acceptance of the gospel. To Arminius, the term "foreknowledge" is an affectionate foreknowledge, but that foreloving cannot be true of the one without Christ. Pinson quoting Arminius,

> "As Arminius perceptively argued, "God can regard no sinner with affection beforehand and love him as His own, unless He has foreknown Him in Christ, and has regarded him as believing upon Christ.... God acknowledges no one from amongst sinners as His own, and loves no one to life eternal, except in Christ and on account of Christ." Thus the word "foreknowledge" also means that God foreknows in the simple sense of prescience, because the only way he can affectionately foreknow people is if he knows them as believers, and to know them as believers, he has to know the fact that they are believers—a fact that he cannot help but know because he is omniscient."[16]

Pinson continues,

> "No one can become conformed to the image of God's son unless he is a believer. The text does not say that God predestined people to belief. It says he predestined those he foreknew as believers to conformity to Christ's image. The only way someone can be conformed to Christ's image is by being in Christ through faith, and since God is consistent in his salvific plan in both time and eternity, he had to have taken individuals' faith into

consideration in eternity. Otherwise, how could he have predestined them to be conformed to Christ's image?"[17]

In his summary of the passage, Pinson states,

> "Verse 29 teaches that those whom God affectionately foreknew in Christ (which means he had to foreknow that they were in Christ by faith) are predestined to conformity to Christ's image. Verse 30 states that these people were also called, justified, and glorified, but it does not deal with two questions: first, whether the nonelect received the same call but resisted it; or second, whether everyone who is justified will also be glorified. The text simply states that those whom God foreknew in Christ from eternity received a call that they did not ultimately reject; thus, they will eventually be glorified. Nothing in the text suggest that God's choice of individuals for eternal salvation is unconditional."[18]

Ephesians and Arminianism

Here we will briefly look at Ephesians and highlight the Arminian position on this text, which gives us principles from the Arminian perspective that can be applied to other texts. The text in question is Ephesians 1:4-11, which reads as follows,

> "even as he chose us in him before the foundation of the world, that we should be holy and blameless before him. In love he predestined us for adoption to himself as sons through Jesus Christ, according to the purpose of his will, to the praise of his glorious grace, with which he has blessed us in the Beloved. In him we have redemption through his blood, the forgiveness of our trespasses, according to the riches of his grace, which he lavished upon us, in all wisdom and insight making known to us the mystery of his will, according to his purpose, which he set forth in Christ as a plan for the fullness of time, to unite all things in him, things in heaven and things on earth." (Ephesians 1:4–10)

In this text, the Arminian will point out that all of the blessings are found in Christ. Because Arminians hold that God's work of predestination occurs "before the foundation of the world," they would maintain that this text doesn't exclude conditional election. The Arminian would say that God's choice of individuals in Christ according to his good pleasure and will (v. 5) doesn't mean that God necessarily chooses without particular conditions that he established. Further, the Arminian would argue that "Indeed, all of God's acts are 'according to the good pleasure of his will.'"[19]

This text indicates to the Arminian that the merit of Christ and all spiritual blessings are apprehended by faith. Instead of being a text of unconditional election it entails conditional election because the text says that God "chose us in him." This understanding that there is no indication of an unconditional election in Ephesians is also applied to other passages.

Calvinists will argue in a similar way, but from the other perspective. They say that the inference of unconditional election is just as reasonable. Calvinists argue that Arminians are loading terms with concepts such as conditions when that cannot be found in the text, making the Arminian deduction less likely.

With that impasse reached, one can now recognize the importance of 'foreknew' in Romans 8 and how it affects one's reading of these texts. While we will get to Romans 8 from the Calvinist position in a moment, we first should look briefly at one major battleground text from the Arminian perspective due to how often it is understood as teaching unconditional election.

Romans 9 and Arminianism

Arminian interpretations of Romans 9 generally have different focuses between them. Most of the focus tends to be on corporate election at the expense of individual election. Thus, in my reliance on Pinson and Forlines, this exposition will be a little unique. Relying on Pinson, who leans in on Leroy Forlines' chapter on Romans 9 in his work Classical Arminianism, we can examine the text and how the Arminian answers the question, "Does Romans 9 teach unconditional election" with a "negative." Forlines, Pinson, and Arminius, see the intent of Paul in Romans 9 is to "show that believers are saved by faith alone, not to teach unconditional election or reprobation."[20] Explaining this,

> "Paul had been preaching that salvation comes through faith in Christ alone, which entailed that most Jews were not part of the covenant. The Jewish response that Paul anticipated was that if God had rejected most of the Jews, God's word or covenant with Abraham was of no effect. According to Arminius, Paul's burden is to show that God's word still stands even if Jews who do not have faith in Christ are excluded from God's promise and blessings, just as some descendants of Abraham and have always been excluded. Thus the question of the text is not whether people are elected unconditionally but whether God's word fails if Jews who seek righteousness by the law instead of faith are excluded from the covenant."[21]

Arminius believes that instead of being about individual election, this text focuses on correcting the notion that many Jews had, that merely being a Jew denoted election. Contrary to this notion, no one is saved by birth or by physical descent. For the Arminian, Paul's argument is focused upon correcting this and pointing out that salvation is not corporate but individual, and that faith is required on the part of the individual to be children of promise rather than children of flesh.

Regarding Paul's discussions around Jacob and Esau in the text, the position is that Paul utilizes them as types, similar to how he does in Galatians 4:21-31 with Ishmael and Isaac. Esau represents a child of the flesh, and Jacob represents a child of promise. Linking the text to Galatians, Paul expresses that those with faith are the children of promise (v. 28). Pinson explains that,

> "Verses 6–13 are not dealing with individual election and reprobation but with Israel's redemptive history. Paul is demonstrating that not all of Abraham's descendants were the covenant descendants of Abraham, and he uses God's choice of Isaac and Jacob and rejection of Ishmael and Esau in the history of redemption to illustrate that fact. This meant that the Jewish people could not claim to be saved based simply on the fact that they were descendants of Abraham.14 Furthermore, God's choice of Jacob over Esau emphasizes God's not basing his choice on anything "good or bad" that they "had done" (9:11). Paul's point here is that salvation is by faith alone, "not because of works" (9:11). Paul reinforces this idea in verse 32, which indicates that the

reason for God's rejection of Israelites is "because they did not pursue it by faith, but as if it were based on works." The church fathers emphasized that God's "loving" of Jacob and "hating" of Esau are conditional, based on divine foreknowledge, which he obviously had before they were born."[22]

In verse 14 of chapter 9, Paul states, "What shall we say then? Is there injustice on God's part? By no means! For he says to Moses, 'I will have mercy on whom I have mercy, and I will have compassion on whom I have compassion." Pinson argues that this line is not about the injustice of God's unconditional election, rather the objection Paul anticipates is that "if God had failed to make good (what they thought was) his promise of the absolute election of all Jews, it would mean that he had failed to keep his word, that he was unjust."[23] Pinson elaborates that Paul is defending God's justice against claims that he would be unjust for not saving all Jews according to the covenant made with Abraham based on physical descent.[24]

> "Paul says that God cannot be unjust and then argues that God's rejection of unbelieving Jews is just, because of the sovereignty of God in salvation. In the next few verses, Paul provides illustrations from Israel's history of God's sovereignty in the plan of salvation to show that God's plan has always been, not a matter of natural descent, nor of the works of the law, but of faith. Paul wants to illustrate two principles: First, God is just in choosing some, but not all, from Israel for salvation.

Second, the Jews are not in a position to argue with God."[25]

The examples that follow verse 14, regarding God's extension of compassion, are not considered a point on God's divine unconditional election, but rather

"The simple question one must ask is: on whom does God desire to show mercy? Paul clearly answers this question in 9:30-33 and the entirety of chapter 19, especially verses 10-2, which detail that he desires to show mercy to Jew and Gentile alike if they will have faith in Jesus the Messiah (10:8-13). Indeed, he is stretching out his hand to beckon Israel to this faith, but they are resisting his gracious call (10:21)."[26]

The point Paul seeks to emphasize is that *God* is the arbiter of what salvation consists of, rather than human beings. Salvation is not by works (i.e., human will and exertion) but by God's grace and mercy. As for the illustration of Pharaoh's hardening of the heart, the argument is that Paul is indicating that mercy is shown to those who do not resist, and yet God will further harden the hearts of those who resist. Yet, Paul in Romans 11 points out that there is still hope for the hardened Jews who can respond in faith to the messiah. Regarding the illustration of the potter and the clay, this refers to the reality that humans have no place to argue against God regarding the terms of salvation. Instead of this giving weight to unconditional election, the argument is that God determines the conditions for salvation. Concerning the language of prepared vessels of wrath and vessels of mercy, Arminius and Pinson state that Romans 9 teaches conditional double predestination.[27]

> "God determined to make people vessels of mercy who should perform the condition of the covenant. Those who should transgress it, and should not desist from transgressing he determined to make vessels of wrath. In essence, Arminius remarked, God makes man a vessel: man makes himself a bad vessel, or sinner: God decrees to make man, according to conditions pleasing to himself, a vessel of wrath or of mercy; which in fact he does, when the condition has been either fulfilled or willfully neglected."[28]

Pinson continues,

> "This gets back to the question: Whom does God will to harden? As Arminius taught, God wills to harden those whom he foreknows will not meet the faith-condition of the covenant: the children of the flesh. On whom does God will to have mercy? The answer is, those whom he foreknows will meet the faith-condition of the covenant: the children of the promise."[29]

Pinson believes Paul's point is to establish that salvation is not by corporate election, Jewish descent, or law keeping, but rather by faith alone.[30] Since salvation is conditioned on faith, and faith is individual, this cannot be corporate election.[31] Instead of affirming the Jewish conception that Jewish people are elect based on their physical descent, Paul's focus is squarely on the faith of individuals in Jesus Christ.[32] Here Paul corrects this conception and shows the Jews that God establishes the way by salvation, and this way is conditional election based on individual faith.[33]

> "Paul uses three illustrations from the history of redemption to argue that the sovereign God alone has the right to set the terms of communion with himself, including his rejection of unbelieving Jews. These illustrations—the hardening of Pharaoh, the potter and the clay, and the vessels of wrath and mercy—do not establish the unconditionality of election but rather underscore Paul's message that it is God, not human beings, who sets the terms of salvation, and this is by faith in the Messiah, not by Jewish descent or law keeping. Most Jews have hardened themselves against God and his anointed one, and God is hardening and blinding them in response, but they still have an opportunity to repent and be saved if they will not resist his loving overtures."[34]

Election and Predestination in Calvinism

As we move into Calvinism on election and predestination, we will follow the same path we laid out when discussing the Arminian position, hitting on the positive case with minimal polemics and focusing on the same texts. We will first revisit where Arminians and Calvinists agree and then explain the Calvinist position of unconditional election. After that, we'll look at the same texts we discussed before, but from the Calvinist perspective.

As mentioned prior, both Classical Arminians and Calvinists agree that God elects people to salvation and also for service. Those elected to salvation are, by extension, called to service. Furthermore, both Calvinists and Arminians typically agree that there is both a corporate and individual aspect to election. As a refresher, the Arminian position argues for conditional election on the basis that salvation is conditioned on believing, and therefore election is conditioned on belief. Man is elect not because God chose him to be elect apart from foreseen faith, but he is elect because God foresaw his faith.

Calvinists, however, hold to unconditional election, which is the position that believes election is God's gracious choice, made in eternity past, to elect a people to be saved by faith through the work of Jesus *without consideration of what man would do*. This choice was not conditional upon any choice this person would make or anything about them - qualities, characters, decision, actions, etc. Instead, it is unconditional. The Calvinist argues that God chooses to love a people because it was his choice, from his will, to give mercy to some and leave others to justice. This election was not because he foreknew what they would do.

Shawn Wright lists a few points on the position that 1) God's election is eternal, 2) Election is Personal, and 3) Election is grounded in God's will, not human choice.[35] These ideas are found in Ephesians 1:3-11.

Addressing point one, Wright directs us to verse 4, "he chose us in him before the foundation of the world." For point two, he looks to verse 4 and 5, emphatic on the point that "we" were predestinated, which is not an abstract group. He then looks to verses 5, 9, 11 for point three "the apostle's exclamations that we were chosen "according to the purpose of his will (v. 5), on the basis of "the mystery of his will...according to his purpose (v.9) and especially that we were predestined "according to the purpose of him who works all things according to the counsel of his will (v.11)" establishes that God's choice, not ours, is the foundation of election.[36] Wright further looks at Acts 13:48 and states the following,

> "Acts 13:48 also teaches unconditional election, for Luke reports that 'as many as were appointed to eternal life believed.' There is no way around the order of thought to arrive at Arminian conclusions. Rather, 'God's appointment of those who would receive eternal life preceded the belief of these very people.' Andrew Davis notes of this verse God is the agent, he ordained or appointed these people for eternal life before the foundation of the world, and as a result of that, they believed the gospel that Paul and Barnabas preached that day. Election is the cause of faith, not the other way around.

Second Timothy 1:9 likewise asserts that God appointed his own to salvation before the ages began."[37]

The Canons of Dort expressly state in 1.9.,

> "this election was not founded upon foreseen faith, and the obedience of faith, holiness, or any other good quality or disposition in man, as the prerequisite, cause or condition on which it depended; but men are chosen to faith and to the obedience of faith, holiness, etc., therefore election is the foundation of every saving good: from which proceed faith, holiness, and the other gives of salvation, and finally eternal life itself."

Further, using Dort as our guide on the topic in article 6, we read,

> "That some receive the gift of faith from God, and others do not receive it, proceeds from God's eternal decree. For known unto God are all his works from the beginning of the world (Acts 15:18). Who worketh all things after the counsel of his will (Eph. 1:11). According to which decree He graciously softens the hearts of the elect, however obstinate, and inclines them to believe; while He leaves the non-elect in His just judgment to their own wickedness and obduracy. And herein is especially displayed the profound, the merciful, and at the same time the righteous discrimination between men equally involved in ruin; or that decree of election and reprobation, revealed in the Word of God, which, though men of perverse, impure, and unstable minds

wrest it to their own destruction, yet to holy and pious souls affords unspeakable consolation."

And article 7,

"Election is the unchangeable purpose of God, whereby, before the foundation of the world, He has out of mere grace, according to the sovereign good pleasure of His own will, chosen from the whole human race, which had fallen through their own fault from their primitive state of rectitude into sin and destruction, a certain number of persons to redemption in Christ, whom He from eternity appointed the Mediator and Head of the elect and the foundation of salvation. This elect number, though by nature neither better nor more deserving than others, but with them involved in one common misery, God has decreed to give to Christ to be saved by Him, and effectually to call and draw them to His communion by His Word and Spirit; to bestow upon them true faith, justification, and sanctification; and having powerfully preserved them in the fellowship of His Son, finally to glorify them for the demonstration of His mercy, and for the praise of the riches of His glorious grace; as it is written: Even as he chose us in him before the foundation of the world, that we should be holy and without blemish before him in love: having foreordained us unto adoption as sons through Jesus Christ unto himself, according to the good pleasure of his will, to the praise of the glory of his grace, which he freely bestowed on us in the Beloved (Eph. 1:4, 5, 6). And elsewhere: Whom he foreordained, them he also called: and whom he called, them he also justified: and whom he justified, them he also glorified (Rom. 8:30)."

In articles 15 and 16, the Canons speak to those who will ultimately be damned, the reprobate. The Canons express that

> "not all have been chosen (to salvation) but that some have not been chosen or have been passed by in God's eternal election – those, that is, concerning whom God, on the basis of his entirely free, most just, irreproachable, and unchangeable good pleasure, made the following decision: to leave them in the common misery into which, by their own fault, they have plunged themselves; not to grant them saving faith and the grace of conversion; but finally to condemn."

Here the Canons express an active election to salvation that necessitates a passing by those who are in sin. This is not equal ultimacy, a notion the Canons reject.

To summarize, Calvinists believe that who God elects and chooses to extend grace and mercy to is entirely his free decision and is not based on anything foreseen in man. Predestination and election are wholly based in God's will not in the will of man or man's future actions. Reprobation (predestination to damnation) in Calvinism is most commonly understood as God passing over individuals and leaving them to justice.

As it was mentioned in chapter 1, the majority of Calvinists would say that 'double predestination' is logically inevitable in any system. Most who push back on 'double predestination' are pushing back on supralapsarianism. While most Calvinists hold to double predestination, they do so with qualification because of the common misconceptions. These qualifications are as follows:

- All men are born totally depraved and on a path to damnation.
- God actively elects those whom he desires to show mercy for salvation.
- God chooses to pass over the non-elect and leaves them to their just end.
- This logically predestines both groups, but this is not equal ultimacy: they are not done in the same way nor equal in importance.

It is worth stating that there are Calvinists who take an approach of an active reprobation and hold to equal ultimacy, though they are fewer. Now we can move on to Romans 8 from a Calvinist viewpoint.

Romans 8:28-30 and Calvinism

Returning to the battleground text of Romans 8:28-30, we will now examine it from the Calvinist perspective. The text reads as follows,

> "And we know that for those who love God all things work together for good, for those who are called according to his purpose. For those whom he foreknew he also predestined to be conformed to the image of his Son, in order that he might be the firstborn among many brothers. And those whom he predestined he also called, and those whom he called he also justified, and those whom he justified he also glorified." (Romans 8:28–30)

As it was highlighted before, the question of this text centers around whether "foreknew" refers to what God knows to be true in the future (he knows who will have faith) or if God foreknew in such a way because he predestined. Put another way, does the verb translated as "foreknew" in this verse indicate prescience (foresight) or foreordination (ordaining something to come to pass beforehand)?

The Calvinist will argue that this verb has the connotation of foreloving, not foresight in the sense of knowing what one will do in the future. Furthermore, the Calvinist believes that this is evident from the passage as a whole. Beginning with the first verse in this passage, we find that God is the one working all things for good, and this is for those who have been called to his purpose. This purpose and plan are expressed in the next couple of verses, with several verbs that, to many commentators, lay out a "golden chain" of salvation, though it's not a complete picture of the doctrine of salvation. The first verb of "foreknow" is crucial for our discussions here. Douglas Moo considers the understanding that puts this verb as "knows beforehand" as unlikely,

> "in the six occurrences of these words in the NT, only two mean "know beforehand"; the three others besides the occurrence in this text, all of which have God as their subject, mean not know before in the sense of intellectual knowledge or cognition, but enter into relationship with before or choose, or determine, before (Romans 11:2; Acts 2:23; 1 Peter 1:2;20). That the verb here contains this peculiarly biblical sense of know is suggested by the fact that it has a simple personal object. Paul does not say that God knew anything about us but that he knew us and this is reminiscent of the OT sense of know. Moreover, it is only some individuals – those who, having been 'foreknown,' were also predestined, called, justified, and glorified – who are the objects of this activity; and this shows that an action applicable only to Christians must be denoted by the verb. If then, the word means know intimately, have regard for, this must be a knowledge or love that is unique to believers and that leads to their being predestined. This being the case, the difference between know or love beforehand and choose beforehand virtually ceases to exist…with the verb, then, Paul highlights the divine initiative in the outworking of God's purpose…

this before does make it difficult to conceive of faith as the ground of this choosing."[38]

Many have noted that the background of foreknowledge is found within the Old Testament, "where the idea (yada) describes God's special knowledge of a person rather than a prior knowledge of how a person will respond to God."[39] Calvinists think this understanding of a special moving into a relationship, intimate knowledge, comes before God's predestining individuals to conform to Christ's image. God foreknows or foreloves the saints themselves, not unbelievers, nor any decision or actions of the saints. Calvinists stress that the text's purpose and context in chapter 8 are for the believer's assurance and to point out how God is working for his will and purpose, while being the subject of every verb in the passage. Because God is working, one can be sure that they will be glorified and that glorification began with foreknowledge.

Ephesians and Calvinism

Ephesians 1:4-11 brings us to an impasse similar to what occurred with Arminians. Both positions argue that their position can be inferred from the text. Calvinists argue that the inference of unconditional election is just as reasonable and requires less loading of terms than the conditional election of Arminianism. The Calvinist, as we noted early in this section, points to the fact that God's election occurs before the foundation of the world, with specific people in mind, and out of God's good will and pleasure. There is no mention of the human's response being the condition by which man is elected. To highlight those again, we can list Wright's points with the corresponding verses in Ephesians:

1. God's election is eternal, verse 4, "he chose us in him before the foundation of the world."
2. Election is Personal, verse 4 and 5 emphatic on the point that "we" were predestinated, not an abstract group.
3. Election is grounded in God's will, not human choice,verses 5, 9, 11, "the apostle's exclamations that we were chosen "according to the purpose of his will (v. 5), on the basis of "the mystery of his will...according to his purpose (v.9) and especially that we were predestined "according to the purpose of him who works all things according to the counsel of his will (v.11)" establishes that God's choice, not ours, is the foundation of election.[40]

Romans 9 and Calvinism

Calvinists say Romans 9 teaches unconditional election, and the Arminian explanations fail to account for all of the data. In this section, we will look at the Calvinist understanding of Romans 9, noting that some details in this exposition may differ between Calvinists.

Prior to this text, Paul has just expressed that the Jews, who the Messiah belonged to, rejected the Messiah when they were God's chosen people. The question is why? At this point, God's promises could be perceived to have failed, as Israel failed to come to Christ. However, Paul counters this in verse 6.

Paul first tells us that the word of God has not failed (v. 6) and explains why we can believe that "For not all who are descended from Israel belong to Israel." The argument is laid out that the word of God has not failed because not all of physical Israel is true Israel. This would have been shocking to the Jews, as they assumed national corporate election, "They thought of themselves as the elect of God and all others as the non-elect. They thought all Jews were going to heaven and all Gentiles to hell."[41]

The reality is that election is only corporate in the sense that God elects individuals into a body and that Gentiles have been included. Paul will, contrary to the Jew's expectations, demonstrate that this is how God has always operated by providing several examples of election, which the Calvinist understands as further expressions of unconditional election. Paul mentions Israel, but emphatically speaks against their ideas of corporate election, saying the nation of Israel was not elected for the promise of salvation, but rather a remnant within Israel was elected to be heirs of the promises. God determined who would be a child of promise and limited his promise to children whom he elected.

Paul further elaborates on his statements that true Israel is actually a remnant within physical Israel, "not all are children of Abraham because they are his offspring, but 'Through Isaac shall your offspring be named. This means that it is not the children of the flesh who are the children of God, but the children of the promises are counted as offspring" (v. 8). Paul's argument is simple: God's promise has not failed because the charge of failure is built on the false premise that merely being a physical descendent makes you an heir of the promise. It must be noted that verse 8 is the focal point of verses 6-13 through Paul's use of a chiasm.

Beginning in verse 6, we read the first distinction between the children of the flesh versus the children of the promise, "For they are not all Israel who are descended from Israel." Verse 7 moves to Isaac, "nor are they all children because they are Abraham's descendants, but 'through Isaac, your descendants will be named," which stresses the same distinction between the children of flesh and those of the promise. The center point of the chiasm is found in verse 8, which reads, "it is not the children of the flesh who are children of God, but the children of the promise who are regarded as descendants." Verse 9 mirrors verse 7 by addressing Isaac again, and verses 10-13 mirror verse 6 by circling back to Jacob. The distinction is made between those who are children of the promise in accordance with God's "purpose of election." This is significant because of the stress put on the phrases "children of God" and "children of the promise." Paul's usage of these phrases elsewhere refers to those who are saved, which can be seen in Romans 8:16 and verse 21, as well as in Philippians 2:15 and Galatians 4:28.

Going back to Paul's examples of election, he first uses the example of Isaac, who would be the child of promise, not Ishmael. The promise did not fail, because only Isaac was the child of promise (v. 9). In Romans 9:10-13, we see another example of God's election in Jacob and Esau, which solidifies God's absolute freedom in election to the Calvinist. They came from the same mother and father, and yet, before they were born, with no account of what they would do, God chose Jacob "in order that God's purpose of election might continue, not because of works but because of him who calls" (v. 11). There was no condition to be met to be elect. Rather, Jacob was elected 'in order that God's purpose of election might continue.' The one who calls, not the one who works, determines election. According to the Calvinist, the structure of verse 11 makes it clear that "God's act of selection is independent of all human effort,"[42] and instead, it is based on God's free, independent, and wise will.

An objection is often raised that Paul is speaking about nations, given Paul's quotation of Genesis 25:23. Yet, Calvinists point out that Paul's quotation stresses Paul's words in verse 6b, "Not all who descended from Israel belong to Israel." Rather than quoting Genesis 25 where it speaks directly about "nations," Paul focuses on the individuals of Jacob and Esau, thus carrying along his theme of a remnant. Furthermore, Paul's stress point in verse 8 regarding the children of the promise as well as his salvific terminology (call and works), points to individuals who are unconditionally elected.

He begins verse 14 by raising another counter-argument, this time regarding the injustice of God that could be perceived on account of his election. Paul responds to this argument of injustice by pointing to the absolute freedom of God to have mercy on whom he desires (v. 15). In this, we see the usage of the terms "mercy" and "compassion," which are verbs describing God's action of choosing whom he will act upon. For the Calvinist, this clearly refers to God's free decision to bestow mercy upon whomever he so wills. "Whom" here is singular, indicating that there are individuals in mind who will be literally "mercied" or "compassioned."

Verse 16 re-stresses God's absolute sovereignty and unconditional election of individuals, "So then it depends not on human will or exertion, but on God, who has mercy," and since conditional election is based upon the human will's cooperation with grace, the Calvinist points to a clear indication of unconditional election. Yes, the election excludes works salvation ("exertion"), but it also excludes dependence upon "human will." Why is God's election fair? Because he is absolutely free in all of his actions to do as he pleases according to his purposes, and neither man's will (repentance and faith are an act of will) nor exertion plays a role. God is God, and can give justice to those who deserve it and have compassion and mercy on those he desires.

Paul demonstrates God's mercy upon individuals and moves the point further by addressing God's sovereignty in Egypt. He points to the reality that it was God's intention to judge Egypt and bring glory to himself through the hardening of Pharaoh's heart (v. 17). Paul then stresses, "So then he has mercy on whomever he wills and he hardens whomever he wills" (v. 18). His last anticipated objection is whether or not man can be held accountable for his response to God, "for who can resist his will" (v. 19). Paul raises the simple point that the created creature is in no position to question how the sovereign potter molds his clay (v. 20) and exercises his freedom. Verse 21 stresses that the potter has the right over his creatures to purpose them for honorable or dishonorable use. The theme of God's absolute sovereignty continues, and as we continue through the text, we read,

> "What if God, desiring to show his wrath and to make known his power, has endured with much patience vessels of wrath prepared for destruction, in order to make known the riches of his glory for vessels of mercy, which he has prepared beforehand for glory" (v. 22-23).

Paul's discussion of God's sovereign and free election to salvation has progressed to showing that there is no charge against God, for he has the complete freedom to do that which he pleases. In 9:22-23, we see that some vessels receive mercy while others are purposed for destruction.

It needs to be mentioned again that the singular is utilized when speaking of a vessel being molded for honor while another is molded for dishonor in verse 21. Furthermore, the usage of "vessel" is always used for individuals, which we see in 1 Thessalonians 4:4, 2

Timothy 2:21, and 1 Peter 3:7. In verses 22-23, we see the term "destruction" used which refers to "annihilation or ruin" while it also refers to final destruction in various other passages. Such destruction cannot be mistaken as anything other than judgment, especially in light of Paul's example of Pharaoh. Additionally, Paul reaffirms the vessels of mercy will be glorified, "prepared beforehand for glory," as he mentioned in the "golden chain" of Romans 8:28-30. Paul moves into the extension of election to the Gentiles in verse 24, in which Paul states, "Even us whom he has called, not from the Jews only but also from the Gentiles."

In summary, like our Arminian exposition before, Romans 9 speaks to individual election and God's sovereignty; however, unlike that exposition, Calvinists view this text as explicitly excluding conditional election as a viable option.

A brief interjection on Romans 9

After briefly outlining the typical articulation from Calvinists on Romans 9, I wanted to present an interjection that relates back to our earlier discussion on Second Temple Judaism and their conceptions of predestination. While this interjection inserts some of my bias into the analysis, I believe it still should be addressed, as it is neglected in most discussions and can be enlightening.[43]

Within Romans 9, Paul alludes to Second Temple Literature, which leans towards a more deterministic articulation of God's sovereignty. Furthermore, as we expressed within our examination of Second Temple Judaism's conceptions of the human will in chapter 3, the Pharisees held to a variety of expressions of compatibilism, to which Paul himself belonged as an exemplary Pharisee. The literature Paul alludes to is the book of Sirach, or the Wisdom of Jesus, Son of Sirach. The literature itself has been deemed by many scholars to be a compatibilistic text akin to the positions held by the Pharisees in that it speaks heavily of God's providence and predestination alongside freewill and moral responsibility. Quoting Robert Wiesner,

> "Sirach 42:15 states that God creates by his powerful word "and all his creatures do his will." Then in 42:19 we read, "[God] declares the things of the past and the things that will be brought to pass and reveals the traces of hidden things" (ἀπαγγέλων τὰ παρεληλυθότα καὶ τὰ ἐσόμενα καὶ ἀποκαλύπτων ἴχνη ἀποκρύφων). This means the creator's "declaration brings the future into

reality." God does not view the future from the outside, but it is his handiwork and will take the shape it does by his design. God's meticulous control over all elements in his creation is strongly emphasized (43:9-26) and is the occasion for the final call to praise (43:27-33). Thus, "the central idea communicated through the hymn is Yhwh's sovereignty over his creation." Or as Perdue says, "The imagery, then, is that of the divine sovereign whose edicts create and rule his kingdom"—which consists of the entire cosmos... [44]

Within Sirach, we find the notion that the potter molds the destinies of all human beings, and that God has an appointment at creation – first, those who will be blessed, exalted, and made near, and second those who will be cursed and brought low. Chapter 33 of Sirach reads as follows,

"All human beings come from the ground, and humankind was created out of the dust. In the fullness of his knowledge the Lord distinguished them and appointed their different ways. Some he blessed and exalted and some he made holy and brought near to himself; but some he cursed and brought low and turned them out of their place. Like clay in the hand of the potter, to be molded as he pleases, so all are in the hand of their maker to be given whatever he decides." (v. 10-13)[45]

Wiesner points out that Sirach presents all things as being the work of God's hand. Ben Sira claims that God has the right in every instance to "fashion some to the exclusion of others for sanctified purposes, without needing justification."[46]

> "Sirach argues that divine election is not random, but is part of a coherent system…context suggests the working of human beings like clay pots (33:13) is about Yahweh's creation of a remnant of faithful individual Israelites (i.e., "the sinner" and "the godly," v. 14) and not the nation in general."[47]

The parallel of this literature with Paul's writing becomes evident, and as well as further parallels which can also be found in Paul's epistle to the Ephesians. Wiesner summarizes the point here,

> "the presence of similar deterministic themes in Sirach, with Paul even showing literary dependence on Sir. 33:7-15 in Romans 9:20-23, demonstrates that divine determinism extended beyond Essenism. Although the predestination language in Paul is perennially debated…[and] because this language is sparse and distinctive in Second Temple Judaism, the correspondences indicate some relationship between the two. The predestinarian language Paul employs suggests that he held to a theology of election remarkably similar to the deterministic ideology identified in Sirach and the Dead Sea Scrolls."[48]

Both the reality that Paul was a Pharisee and that he utilized a text that closely aligns with conceptions of the Pharisee's position on human freedom should be considered on the subject when discussing the text. It helps frame where Paul is writing from, which leads us to an interpretation based on authorial intent. While it is tempting to dismiss this reference by Paul, it may give significant insight into Paul's theology of sovereignty about freedom.

Summary

Calvinists and Arminians both believe in election and predestination that occurs before the foundation of the world. Generally, there is also agreement that election is both individual and corporate while also being election to service and salvation. However, the views diverge where Calvinists hold to unconditional election, whereby man's future choices have no bearing on God's predestination and election. In contrast, the Arminian holds to conditional election where the condition of accepting faith must be met to be predestined and one of the elect.

Chapter 7
The Atonement: its Extent and Otherwise

Introduction: Misconceptions and Agreements

In many ways, the discussion on the atonement will be easier than our previous discussions because of how the atonement fits into each system. Chapters seven and eight of this book will be relatively straight forward because the doctrines in question are logically linked to components we have already discussed. In other words, limited atonement makes sense in Calvinism, and unlimited atonement makes sense in Arminianism. The Calvinist understanding of atonement and eternal security are bound together with the Calvinist understanding of predestination and compatibilism.

Before beginning, however, it must also be said that there are works entirely dedicated to these last two subjects we are discussing. It is important to remember that our discussions here do not exhaust the arguments for each position. We are succinctly addressing points of agreement and disagreement on these doctrines.

More time will be spent on the Calvinist position in this section to articulate the differing conceptions of limited atonement. We will focus more on the positive cases for each position and less on the polemics. While our key distinction between Arminianism and Calvinism will be highlighted, discussing misconceptions and agreements between the two is also essential.

The first point of agreement between Calvinists and Arminians is that the atonement is always limited *in its application*. Whether the atonement is unlimited or limited is not a debate on whether or not the atonement is applied to every individual leading to universalism (the idea that all people are ultimately saved). Instead, the debate is centered around the question: when Christ died, who did he die for?

In both positions, the application of the atonement is only upon the elect, and is linked to those who exercise faith. Arminians holding that Christ made atonement available to all via unlimited atonement is not the same as what universalists say, which is that the atonement is applied (whether now or eventually) to all individuals. In both systems, there is a sense in which the atonement is limited, but in a different measure. While Calvinists critique unlimited atonement by stating that it implies or logically leads to universalism, Arminians disagree. Generally, both Calvinists and Arminians agree that universalism is heresy.

Another point that needs to be addressed is that in literature, Arminians are usually labeled as holding to 1) a governmental theory of atonement, and 2) a rejection of the imputation of Christ's righteousness. While some

Wesleyan Arminians may reject the imputation of Christ's righteousness in justification, Reformed or Classical Arminians do not. Jacob Arminius and the Remonstrance held to the typical Reformed doctrine of imputation, which the English General Baptists carried along.

Regarding the first point, Matthew Pinson states the following,

> "Contrary to popular belief, Arminius did not teach a governmental view of atonement, despite the fact that so many subsequent Arminians have. Instead, he held fast to the Reformed view of penal substitutionary atonement articulated in the Belgic Confession and Heidelberg Catechism. This view sees Christ's priestly sacrifice as a necessary response to human sinfulness and the inflexible justice of God, which cannot be set aside without doing damage to the divine essence. For Arminius, as for most other Reformed theologians of his day, God, by means of Christ's propitiatory sacrifice, extends his mercy to sinners while satisfying his justice. Through his oblation, Christ as priest and sacrifice suffers the divine punishment that is due for human sin. This suffering constitutes the satisfaction or payment to the divine justice for redemption of human beings from sin, guilt, and wrath. Arminius's understanding of the nature of atonement, in the context of his view of the priestly office of Jesus Christ, beautifully expresses the penal-substitutionary views of the Reformed theology of his day."[1]

Our concern here, however, is less on these other issues and rather on the *extent* of the atonement. Did Christ die and atone only for the sins of the elect or for everyone in the world? Was the intent of the atonement to save only the elect or to provide salvation for all?

Arminians on the Atonement

Logically following the Arminian conception of human will and universal prevenient grace comes the position of universal or unlimited atonement. The Father is drawing everyone, the Son died for everyone, and the Holy Spirit is calling everyone to salvation. Because God desires all to be saved, a provision must be provided for that to be possible, and thus Christ died for the sins of everyone.

However, the application of this provision/atonement is limited to those who do not resist grace. Amidst the Calvinist critique that God had the Son to die for everyone, including those he foreknew before the world existed would reject him, Arminians seek to maintain the free offer of the gospel to everyone. Arminians point out that there are no scriptures that imply the notion that Christ died only for the sins of the elect and say there simply are no texts for the Calvinist to bring to the table. The Arminian points to a number of texts indicating Jesus died for all or the whole world, which are texts Calvinists have to wrestle with in their framework.

We will now survey some of these texts here from the Arminian perspective. First, in John's literature, the "world" is emphasized. Because it is often used to indicate the unbelieving world, especially in contrast to those who believe, we find a universal love of God in texts such as John 3:16. An example of this is in 1 John 5:19, "We know that we are from God, and the whole world lies in the power of the evil one" where there is a clear distinction. Yet John 3:16 states, "God so loved the world, that he gave his only Son, that whoever believes in him should not perish but have eternal life."

Prior to this verse, we read of Moses and the bronze serpent (v. 14), wherein this serpent is provided for everyone in Moses' presence and applied to those who would look at it. Furthermore, John the Baptist calls Jesus the Lamb of God who takes away the sin of the world (John 1:29). John calls Jesus the savior of the world in a handful of texts, but 1 John 2:2 states, "He is the propitiation for our sins, and not for ours only but also for the sins of the whole world." Arminians reject the conception put forward by Calvinists that" world" often designates all kinds of people and point to these texts that define the world as those who lie in the power of the evil one (1 John 5:19). Hebrews 2:9 states that Christ "tasted death for everyone" and Arminians point out that in 2 Peter 2:1 false teachers are bought by the Lord, having been atoned for, but ultimately lost.

This universal atonement makes salvation possible for everyone, but is only actualized when individuals accept it through repentance and faith. Calvinists challenge this in a number of ways, but two are as follows: first, Calvinists state that Arminians limit the power of the atonement, as there are a number of individuals Jesus died for that he ultimately fails to save. They add that this universal atonement is needless when God foreknows who will choose him before the foundation of the world. Second, Calvinists often note that the sin of unbelief would be atoned for on the cross for every individual, logically entailing universalism since unbelief is the sin that keeps individuals from being saved. Arminians respond to point

The Atonement: its Extent and Otherwise

one by saying that the Calvinist makes a false conflation of the atonement *accomplished* and the atonement *applied*. To the latter point, Arminians point out that there needs to be an active apprehension of faith and union with Christ to be saved. These two points are not the only points of debate on the subject, but are some that appear often in discussions.

Calvinists on the Atonement

Within the Reformed Tradition, there are three positions on the atonement. 1) Christ died only for the elect and in no way whatsoever for the non-elect, 2) Christ died especially for the elect, and there is a general aspect for all men, and lastly, 3) Christ died equally for all men. The third category would be considered "4 Point Calvinism." Sometimes the first position is called "strict limited atonement," and position two is called "moderate limited atonement."

Where Dort and other confessions fall tends to be debated, but as Curt Daniel notes, they lean towards strict limited atonement while allowing for a moderate limited atonement.[2] For example, the Canons of Dort under the second head of doctrine, article 3 states,

> "The death of the Son of God is the only and most perfect sacrifice and satisfaction for sin; is of infinite worth and value, abundantly sufficient to expiate the sins of the whole world."[3]

Articles 8 and 9 state,

> "For this was the sovereign counsel and most gracious will and purpose of God the Father, that the quickening and saving efficacy of the most precious death of his Son should extend to all the elect, for bestowing upon them alone the gift of justifying faith, thereby to bring them infallibly to salvation: that is, it was the will of God, that Christ by the blood of the cross, whereby he

confirmed the new covenant, should effectually redeem out of every people, tribe, nation, and language, all those, and those only, who were from eternity chosen to salvation, and given to him by the Father; that he should confer upon them faith, which, together with all the other saving gifts of the Holy Spirit, he purchased for them by his death; should purge them from all sin, both original and actual, whether committed before or after believing; and having faithfully preserved them even to the end, should at last bring them free from every spot and blemish to the enjoyment of glory in his own presence forever.

This purpose proceeding from everlasting love towards the elect, has, from the beginning of the world to this day, been powerfully accomplished, and will, henceforward, still continue to be accomplished, notwithstanding all the ineffectual opposition of the gates of hell; so that the elect in due time may be gathered together into one, and that there never may be wanting a Church composed of believers, the foundation of which is laid in the blood of Christ, which may steadfastly love and faithfully serve him as their Saviour, who, as a bridegroom for his bride, laid down his life for them upon the cross; and which may celebrate his praises here and through all eternity "[4]

Additionally, Calvinists debate whether some figures, such as Calvin himself, held to a moderate (2) or universal view (3). For example, on Galatians 5:12, Calvin said, "It is the will of God that we should seek the salvation of all men without exception, as Christ suffered for the sins of the whole world."[5] On Colossians 1:14 he said, "By the sacrifice of his death all the sins of the world have been expiated."[6]

Yet, Daniel points out that the moderate limited atonement, as opposed to the strict view, appears to be the mainline position – holding that there is a universal aspect for all men though Christ died primarily for the elect.[7] Daniel demonstrates this in Edwards, Spurgeon, Baxter, Ryle, Martyn Lloyd-Jones, and so forth,[8] noting that they stress that Christ died for all men, but especially the elect. As many in the tradition would state, "Christ died sufficiently for all, but efficaciously only for the elect." What this universal aspect is differs among the tradition. However, many link it to the general call where it is the grounds for a genuine free gospel offer, common grace, and especially the effects of the atonement on all of creation culminating into the New Heavens and New Earth.

Moving on from here, we find there is a close relationship between election, predestination, and this atonement. God has chosen who will be saved, and God has worked in history to affect his will; the atonement does not need to go beyond the elect. The elect are known and do not increase or decrease in number.

The Calvinist points to Ephesians 1 in demonstrating how closely God's election and the atonement are for the purposes of making a holy and blameless people. The atonement is the means by which God brings about his purpose of saving his people. While God has a general love for all his creatures, there is a special love for Christ's bride that is not given to those who are not Christ's bride.

Calvinists also point to texts such as John 10:11, which we examined in chapter four, where Jesus says, "I am the good shepherd. The good shepherd gives his life for the sheep." According to verses 12 and 26, the unbelievers who are not of his sheep will not have his life on their behalf. The shepherd does not give his life for goats or wolves, but for those sheep he knows and who know his voice.

The moderate position typically utilizes the language of 1 Timothy 4:10, "For to this end we toil and strive, because we have our hope set on the living God, who is the savior of all people, especially of those who believe." The Calvinist says Christ's death has a purpose and guarantees success as he secured the elect's salvation. Because Christians agree with the limited application of the atonement to those who have faith, looking at the texts where the apostles stress that saints have been saved via the work of the cross is not necessary for our purposes.

When it comes to objections such as the false teachers who are bought in 2 Peter 2:1, and texts that speak about Christ's dying for all or the world, Calvinists have a variety of answers. In the moderate limited atonement view, the solution is much simpler than in the strict position since the moderate position allows one to affirm both a universal and particular scope of the atonement. Yet, it is also noted that "all" in each text does not necessarily mean every person without exception. The term can be limited in context, such as those in the Roman Empire when Caesar summoned "all" for a census, or "all" kinds of people, such as Jews and Gentiles. In Mark 1:5, we read of "all" in the land of Judea and Jerusalem going out to hear John the Baptist and being baptized by him, yet we know this isn't every person without exception, as even Luke 7:30 notes that John did not baptize the Pharisees. This is to say that the Calvinist takes each text on a case-by-case basis but points out that saying "all means all" is insufficient on its own.

In the case of texts such as 1 John 2:2, which many consider the Achilles heel of limited atonement, answers vary. However, Calvinists point out that 'world' can also be limited in what is being referenced, especially in John's literature, where the apostle utilizes the term in several ways. On 1 John, Calvinists from a more strict limited perspective argue from a number of angles, though those of the moderate position have little to quarrel with on the point.

Summary

On the position of the atonement, we find more variance in the Calvinist position than in the Arminian position, yet, the mainline distinction is that Christ died equally for all men in the same way vs. Christ died for all men in some way, but he died particularly or effectively only for the elect. Both of these positions flow from the two system's other points we have discussed so far. The extent of the atonement becomes a domino later in the line, which is why many Calvinists consider 4-point Calvinism inconsistent. That said, many individuals who claim the title of 4-point Calvinism will utilize the same scriptural arguments as Arminians for universal atonement. Typically, once individuals align with Calvinism or Arminianism on grace, the will, and predestination, they'll find their position on the atonement quickly following.

Chapter 8
Perseverance of the Saints

Much like our discussion on the atonement, comparing and contrasting Arminianism and Calvinism on eternal security, or perseverance of the saints, is relatively clear-cut because of how the topic logically fits into each system. While Calvinism had more variation on the atonement than Arminianism, the Arminians have more variation on this particular topic. This section essentially addresses the question, "can we lose our salvation?" We'll begin with the Calvinist position first because of the uniformity on the topic.

Calvinism on Eternal Security

The P in TULIP stands for Perseverance of the Saints, sometimes called the Preservation of the Saints. The Westminster Confession summarizes the point as follows,

> "They whom God hath accepted in his beloved, effectually called and sanctified by his Spirit, can neither totally nor finally fall away from the state of grace; but shall certainty persevere therein to the end and be eternally saved" (17.1)

It is this idea of God's preservation and the saint's perseverance in the faith that distinguishes Calvinism from the popular position of "once saved, always saved." This position of eternal security is grounded in the doctrines covered previously. In reading texts like Romans 8 again, we find that those whom God foreknew will be called, justified, and ultimately glorified. Part of Paul's argument in Romans 8 is that nothing can separate us from God's love, and God has indeed predestined us to glorification or conformity to Christ's image. Philippians 1:6 says, "he who began a good work in you will bring it to completion at the day of Jesus Christ." Calvinists also go back to texts such as John 6 where we read,

> "All that the Father gives me will come to me, and whoever comes to me I will never cast out. For I have come down from heaven, not to do my own will but the will of him who sent me. And this is the will of him who

sent me, that I should lose nothing of all that he has given me, but raise it up on the last day." (John 6:37–39)

All those that the Father gives to the Son will not be lost but instead raised and glorified on the last day. A similar sentiment is expressed in John 10:27-30,

> "My sheep hear my voice and I know them, and they follow me. I give them eternal life, and they will never perish and no one will snatch them out of my hand. My Father, who has given them to me, is greater than all, and no one is able to snatch them out of my Father's hand. I and the Father are one."

Paul likewise states that the Lord Jesus Christ will sustain the saints until the end (1 Cor. 1:4-8), and that they have a guarantee of their redemption in the Holy Spirit, their seal (Eph. 1:13-14). Bavinck on this point states,

> "The question is not whether believers on their own can maintain or lose their faith; the question is whether God upholds, continues, and completes the work of grace he has begun, or whether he sometimes permits it to be totally ruined by the power of sin."[1]

The Calvinist places salvation and the work of salvation wholly in the hands of the redeemer. Bavinck continues,

> "Perseverance is not an activity of the human person but a gift from God. Among the Reformed the doctrine

of perseverance is seen as a gift of God who assures that the work of grace is continued and completed, which he does through believers. In regeneration and faith, he grants a grace that as such bears an inadmissible character; he grants a life that is by nature eternal; he bestows the benefits of calling, justification, and glorification that are mutually and unbreakably interconnected."[2]

The Westminster Confession of Faith, on Perseverance states the following on the doctrine,

"They whom God hath accepted in his Beloved, effectually called and sanctified by his Spirit, can neither totally nor finally fall away from the state of grace; but shall certainly persevere therein to the end, and be eternally saved.

This perseverance of the saints depends, not upon their own freewill, but upon the immutability of the decree of election, flowing from the free and unchangeable love of God the Father; upon the efficacy of the merit and intercession of Jesus Christ; the abiding of the Spirit and of the seed of God within them; and the nature of the covenant of grace: from all which ariseth also the certainty and infallibility thereof.

Nevertheless they may, through the temptations of Satan and of the world, the prevalency of corruption remaining in them, and the neglect of the means of their preservation, fall into grievous sins; and for a time continue therein: whereby they incur God's displeasure, and grieve his Holy Spirit; come to be deprived of some measure of their graces and comforts; have their hearts hardened, and their consciences wounded; hurt and scandalize others, and bring temporal judgments upon themselves."[3]

The Westminster Confession compliments Bavinck's point that perseverance is God's gift and his work in believers. The confession also points out that there are times when men can fall into periods of "grievous sins," yet they can "neither totally nor finally fall away from the state of grace; but shall certainly persevere therein to the end, and be eternally saved."

While this is God's preservation, the Calvinists position on compatibilism does not negate sanctification - growing in holiness. In fact, the Calvinist believes God's working in man necessitates sanctification. Quoting part of article 24 of the Belgic Confession we read,

"We believe that this true faith, being wrought in man by the hearing of the Word of God and the operation of the Holy Ghost, doth regenerate and make him a new man, causing him to live a new life, and freeing him from the bondage of sin.

Therefore it is so far from being true, that this justifying faith makes men remiss in a pious and holy life, that on the contrary without it they would never do any thing out of love to God, but only out of self-love or fear of damnation.

Therefore it is impossible that this holy faith can be unfruitful in man: for we do not speak of a vain faith, but of such a faith as is called in Scripture a faith that worketh by love, which excites man to the practice of those works which God has commanded in his Word."[4]

The Confession points out that because it is God working in man, and because he has made man a 'new man,' the redeemed will produce fruit. It is God working in these individuals so that individuals do not become cold toward living in holiness, but instead moves the redeemed into obedience. The article is quick to point out that these works are not meritorious, but instead that assurance rests on the person and work of Jesus Christ.

This all brings out the reality that Christians are responsible to continue and persevere in Christ. This call to persevere is echoed in the New Testament in various ways, especially in the warning passages. However, a few questions come to mind about eternal security in the Calvinistic framework. 1) How do we understand those warning passages that seem to imply one can indeed lose their salvation? 2) What of those who are apostates? And 3) How is it distinct from "once saved, always saved"?

In response to question one, there are a number of answers within the Reformed tradition, but I will briefly provide one perspective. This perspective is that the warning passages in scripture are addressed to believers, who are threatened with eternal destruction if they commit apostasy. While genuine believers won't commit apostasy, the texts are predominately for them and are a means by which God brings about perseverance: diligence, renewed faith, self-examination, and so forth.

This view is found in individuals such as Spurgeon, Owen, Bavinck, Berkhof, Calvin, and many others. In his systematic notes, Louis Berkhof says, "Warnings do not prove that any of the addressed will apostatize, but simply that the use of means is necessary to prevent them from committing this sin."[5] Bavinck similarly notes,

> "All of the above-mentioned admonitions and threats that scripture addresses to believers, therefore, do not prove a thing against the doctrine of perseverance. They are rather the way in which God himself confirms his promise and gift through believers. They are the means by which perseverance in life is realized."[6]

For question two, the answer is found in the reality that not all Christians are actually Christians. We see this idea with the false prophets in Matthew 7:21-23, but especially in 1 John. 1 John 2:18-19 says that apostates and false teachers "went out from us, but they were not of us; for if they had been of us, they would have continued with us. But they went out, that it might become plain that they all are not of us." Shawn Wright on this passage, states,

> "John does not say that these false teachers lose their faith. Rather, he reasons in a ex post facto manner. Their abandonment of the fellowship proves that they were never truly part of the church."[7]

For question three, the answer is that generally, "once saved, always saved" focuses upon God's preservation of his people at the expense of the reality that Christians will persevere until the end or produce fruit. Usually, the phrase "once saved, always saved" to modern ears means something akin to a one-and-done confession, altar call, profession of faith, etc., with no evidence of a changed life affected by union with Christ. Historically, the Reformed tradition has stressed the importance of *possessing* faith rather than a *profession* without possession. Furthermore, Calvinists stress the living nature of faith and reject the idea of a category of Christian that is 'carnal' yet somehow saved. As noted before, while the Calvinistic Confessions point out that a Christian can fall into a period of grievous sins, they will be restored if their conversion is genuine.[8]

Ultimately, the Calvinist position is that those who have been predestined will be glorified, and that God is working in believers to will and to work for his good pleasure. Those who have apostatized were never Christians to begin with, but rather false professors who may have 'tasted' the Holy Spirit via being in a Christian community. The Calvinist position is logically in step with the other points of TULIP, but also seeks to stress that man cannot lose that which was never his to earn, i.e., salvation. From beginning to end, salvation is brought about by God's grace and plan to save a people for himself.

Arminianism on Eternal Security

Arminians differ on the point of eternal security amongst themselves to some extent. Here we will summarize Matthew Pinson's articulations on Classical Arminianism, which appears to be the majority position. Pinson critiques those who wish to uphold libertarian freedom and eternal security as being inconsistent, and instead points out that there is an affirmation of God's preservation of the saints, or eternal security of the believer. However, like election, it is conditional upon one's status as a believer. In other words, those who persevere remain believers and have eternal security, but could also leave the faith and cease believing. There is no guarantee that they will persevere until the end. However, as long as they remain in union with Christ through faith, believers are righteous in him.[9]

In Arminianism, the warning passages and their conditional clauses of "if" you continue, endure, overcome, you will be saved are important to this understanding. Those passages that Calvinists will utilize for eternal security, for the Arminian, are conditional upon one's remaining in union with Christ. Pinson, however, emphasizes that this is not a maintaining of works and he critiques some "works-oriented Arminianism." The condition to be met is remaining in Christ for salvation, not seeking to earn righteousness via works. Pinson states,

> "The best way to get beyond the divide between Calvinists and Arminians on perseverance and apostasy is to emphasize continuing in the righteousness of Christ

alone through faith alone. This Reformed Arminian posture is preferable to an Arminian approach that emphasizes continuing intermittently in faith-plus-lawkeeping or an eternal securitist posture that emphasizes relying on a past decision that cannot be reversed. That Reformed Arminian approach alone does justice to the warning passages, which warn believers to continue in faith lest they fall from grace, as well as the promise passages, which assure believers of their security in Christ alone if they continue in faith alone."[10]

For Pinson, Arminians who hold to eternal security, as well as Calvinists, are importing the notion into the text. Yet, the text never guarantees that those who take hold of faith will continue in that faith indefinitely. Pinson believes this is clear in the warning passages, which imply the opposite. In responding to the notion that "if we could lose our salvation, there would be no assurance of salvation," Pinson simply answers that assurance is in the person and work of Christ and our union with him, not the promise that we won't apostatize. He observes,

"When responding to theological and logical arguments by Calvinists, Arminians readily grant that if Calvinists can prove that God absolutely destines people for salvation unconditionally and draws them irresistibly to it, then certain perseverance logically follows and theologically fits. Thus the argument between classical Calvinists and Arminians is always going to go back to the other points of Calvinism."[11]

To the Arminian that rejects eternal security, the warning passages are clear enough to establish that Christians can be genuinely united to Christ and then leave the faith. Yet, Pinson also speaks briefly about two types of apostasy that some Arminians articulate. The first is total and final apostasy, which is reckoned as rare and severe. This type of apostasy is a renouncing of belief which cannot be remedied. The second type of apostasy is backsliding, which is considered more common and occurs through sinning. Pinson states that Reformed Arminians tend to hold to only one kind of apostasy, the first kind.[12]

This first kind of apostasy is spoken of in Hebrews 6, 10, Matthew 12:31, and other scriptures. Other Arminians - those who are not Reformed Arminians - believe the second kind of Apostasy is caused by unconfessed sin, and repentance is the key to eternal security in this view. Pinson argues that this type of apostasy is not found in scripture and instead that scripture only presents one type of falling away. Furthermore,

> "They argue that justification by faith is a one-for-all category that incorporates the believer into a status of being in Christ rather than a fragile possession one is carrying in one's hands. Third, they argue that Apostasy 2 is an implicit denial of the doctrine of justification by the imputed righteousness of Christ appended through faith.... Justifying faith does not come and go, wax and wane, as believers' sin and receive forgiveness for their sins. That is the way many Arminians see justifying faith. They think that, when an unbeliever gets into a condition of unconfessed sin, that indicates the absence

of faith. Thus, again, for many Arminians, justification is more like a substance one possesses rather than a forensic status into which one is incorporated. Reformed Arminians do not view justifying faith and its relation to sin in the believer's life in this way. Rather, they see justification by faith as a decisive, once-for-all status into which the believer is incorporated. Thus, even when believers are in a condition of sin of which they have not repented, they remain in union with Christ, they retain their "in Christ" status (1 Peter 1:5). Their justifying faith is still intact, which maintains their union with Christ. Union with Christ is a status into which the believer has been incorporated. As long as the believer is in union with Christ, his or her sins are covered."[13]

Ultimately, because Reformed Arminians hold to the same principles as Calvinists on justification and faith, they reject the notion that sinning and failing to repent affects one's status with God. Thus, because justification is by faith and not maintained by works for the Reformed Arminian, there is only one type of apostasy: a total renouncing of faith and no longer being united to the person and work of Christ.

Summary

Calvinists and Arminians agree that salvation is by faith alone in Christ alone. Both groups also agree that eternal security is tied to the person and work of Jesus Christ and his perfect obedience. They also agree that God is working in us to make us more like Christ. Our works do not increase or decrease our justification, but can act as a confirmation of it. Furthermore, we are not saved by our works, but solely by the work of Christ. Fruit and perseverance until glorification will be present in those who are in Christ.

However, in Arminianism, man can resist God's working within him and detach himself from Christ, his eternal security. Because of this, man can lose his salvation which is tied to that union with Jesus. Calvinists, on the other hand, are emphatic on the point that God will see his work completed and that individuals cannot lose salvation. While they may stray for a time, they will inevitably persevere in the faith via God's grace and power.

Chapter 9
Conclusion

As we conclude our comparison and contrast of Classical Arminianism and Calvinism, I hope that some strawmen have been burned down and key points of agreement can now lend themselves to more meaningful future discussions. In many ways, a lot of the same practical concerns arise in Arminians and Calvinism, especially against the modern evangelicals' tendency towards works-righteousness and Pelagianism. It is on these points of agreement that Calvinists and Arminians should happily find common ground and speak out with a unified voice saying, "It is by grace that salvation begins, works out, and ends." Although we only scratched the surface of the many disagreements between the different systems, they can be discussed respectfully.

As it was prefaced in this volume, we all know the topic of Calvinism vs. Arminianism sparks heated debates. In most of these discussions, you'll find less than fruitful interactions. Despite how off-putting this may be for those who want to engage in the topic, I'd encourage

Christians to still work through it as the subject *will* impact how you view the Christian experience.

Despite my bias toward Calvinism coming through at points, I hope this proves to be a balanced resource on critical issues. While I am ultimately unconvinced of Arminianism, I have grown to greatly appreciate Reformed Arminians, Reformed Weslyeans, and the Society of Evangelical Arminians in particular. This book certainly does not give you every detail of the two positions, and I'm sure some of the chapters left you 'hungry for more.' Still, this volume provides you somewhere to start when considering how you think through these topics (*see Appendix E*). Most importantly, I hope this book leads you to scripture as you consider these subjects.

To conclude, I want to remind the reader of the two myths raised in the discussion of Calvinism and Arminianism. First, is that Arminianism and Calvinism are opposites. And secondly is the myth that a hybrid of Calvinism and Arminianism is possible. The first polarizes, and the second naively attempts to unify. It should be evident why these are indeed myths. There is a sense of continuity, especially historically, as both find their key battleground together in the Netherlands, but also a reality of discontinuity. While Calvinism and Arminianism can sometimes seem to be saying the same things with different terms and emphasis, we must remember that they are different enough that a hybrid is simply impossible, as they are classically defined and articulated.

What is possible, however, is a recognition of unity in our blessed redeemer Jesus Christ and an extension of table fellowship. We must remember that we hold and profess the same gospel and the same Christ. The intricate details of *how* salvation works should not be a point of division in terms of whether or not we consider one a brother or sister in Christ. So long as we can affirm that we are saved by faith alone in Christ alone unto the glory of God alone, we can continue to proclaim Christ's death, burial, and resurrection together.

Classical Calvinism and Classical Arminianism Compared:

Doctrine/Topic	Classic Calvinism	Classic Arminianism
Original Sin	Yes	Yes
Original Guilt	Yes [majority]	Some
Total Depravity	Yes	Yes
Total inability	Yes	Yes
Call of God	There is a general call to salvation for all that is resisted by the natural man and there is an effectual call given to the elect that is effectual.	There is a universal call of salvation for all that can be resisted or embraced by the enablement of God's grace.
Special [salvific] Grace	Is particular - given to the elect.	Universal [different positions on means of how this grace is distributed]
Salvific Grace	Is effectual or irresistible: the elect will inevitably come to Christ	Is resistible: man can resist this special grace and reject Christ
Faith	Faith is a gift from God	Faith is a gift from God
Regeneration	Regeneration is a work of God that comes logically prior to faith (for most Calvinists)	Regeneration is a work of God that logically comes after faith.
God Elects to	Both Salvation and Service	Both Salvation and Service
Election is	Both Individual and Corporate	Both Individual and Corporate
Election/Predestination is	Unconditional - not based on man's choices, but based on God's choice	Conditional - election is conditioned on the belief of the individual.
Foreknowledge is	Foreloving/Foreordination - Choosing to enter into a relationship with individuals	Foreloving/Foresight of those believers who will be in Christ [can have different positions on foreknowledge]
The Atonement is	Limited in its Application to the elect	Limited in its Application to the elect
Christ died for	Only the Elect (or) Everyone but 'especially the elect.' The atonement's application is apprehended by faith.	Everyone. The atonement's application is apprehended by faith.
Eternal Security	Those elected by God will ultimately and finally be glorified - they will be preserved by God and persevere in the faith [contra 'once saved always saved'].	Those who remain united to Christ have eternal security based on Christ's righteousness. These individuals however can leave the faith. Eternal Security is conditional upon union with Christ [not works].
Warning Passages	Warning passages are a means of grace to bring about perseverance (one of the views).	Are passages that speak to the reality that believers can and (some) will fall away.
Apostates	Are those who were never genuinely saved.	Some may be false converts, but apostates can be those who genuinely left the faith.

Appendix A: What does "Reformed" mean?

This question arises reasonably often and has a more convoluted answer than one may expect. For example, we encounter Lutherans who are not considered "Reformed," yet we know Luther was a Reformer! Furthermore, we see an influx of Classical Arminians taking on their Reformed roots and calling themselves Reformed Arminians. What makes things even more confusing is when the Calvinists, who are often considered Reformed, will say that some other Calvinist is not "Reformed." What are we to make of this?

The reality is that the term Reformed can be a bit more fluid than most would expect. Ligonier Ministries plainly states, "The question (what does it mean to be reformed] does not have a clear-cut answer. The word has a more inclusive definition as well as a less inclusive definition."[1]

In its most broad sense, being reformed designates a branch of the Reformation Era, often beginning with Zwingli, who differed from the Lutherans during the Reformation. While Luther was a reformer, the Lutherans were distinguished from the "Reformed" churches very early on. This distinction is standard and made by Lutherans and the Reformed alike to this day.

This Reformed tradition would eventually be marked by those holding to the original two forms of unity: the Belgic Confession and the Heidelberg Catechism. This standard of being Reformed included the Arminians but excluded Particular (Calvinistic) Baptists. Some will point to these Reformed roots for claiming the designation of "Reformed Arminianism," especially due to Arminius and the Remonstrance's continued subscription to the standard mentioned above. To this day, the Remonstrant Brotherhood of the Netherlands is included in the World Communion of Reformed Churches.

While the World Communion of Reformed Churches includes these Arminians, the events at the Synod of Dort would eliminate Arminians from that designation. This is because, for most, the two forms of unity would become three by including the Canons of Dort, which would exclude any Arminian adherents.

While not under this strict category, the Westminster Standards (the Confession and Catechisms) are also often considered Reformed. Further complicating the matter were the Reformed or Particular Baptists, who sprung from the independent Paedobaptists (Puritans). For many, the differences in views between Baptists and Paedobaptists on the subject of baptism have excluded Baptists from the designation of being "Reformed."

The most common modern designation of what it means to be reformed are the three "Cs." This includes being covenantal, confessional, and Calvinistic. This

Appendix A: What does "Reformed" mean?

means you can be a Calvinist without being Reformed (for example, John MacArthur, who is Calvinist but also a dispensationalist). It also means you can be confessional without being Reformed (such as with the Arminians).

The most inclusive model of what it means to be Reformed, then, would include the Particular Baptists and the Westminster Standards. This would make the three Cs the standard for what it means to be Reformed. The more exclusive model (Belgic, Heidelberg, Dort) would, by necessity, exclude the Baptists but still include the Westminster Standards. Both common conceptions generally exclude Arminians.

Regardless of those details, the key stressing point could be boiled down to this: Reformed does not equal Calvinist. Reformed may encompass Calvinistic doctrines, but they are not synonymous. Furthermore, it doesn't matter in particular whether you are Reformed in your theological tradition, but instead, whether you are being re-formed in Christ.

Appendix B: Council of Orange

The Council and Canons of Orange contain significant overlap with obvious texts in scripture that spoke to the fallen nature of humanity but expanded on anthropology and soteriology in order to combat semi-Pelagianism.

Philip Schaff summarizes the five propositions:

1. Through the fall free will has been so weakened, that without prevenient grace no one can love God, believe on Him, or do good for God's sake, as he ought (*sicut oportuit*, implying that he may in a certain measure).
2. Through the grace of God all may, by the co-operation of God, perform what is necessary for their soul's salvation.
3. It is by no means our faith, that any have been predestinated by God to sin (*ad malum*), but rather: if there are people who believe so vile a

thing, we condemn them with utter abhorrence (*cum omni detestatione*).[1892]
4. In every good work the beginning proceeds not, from us, but God inspires in us faith and love to Him without merit precedent on our part, so that we desire baptism, and after baptism can, with His help, fulfil His will.
5. Because this doctrine of the fathers and the synod is also salutary for the laity, the distinguished men of the laity also, who have been present at this solemn assembly, shall subscribe these acts.[1]

Relevant Declarations from the Canons:[2]

CANON 4. If anyone maintains that God awaits our will to be cleansed from sin, but does not confess that even our will to be cleansed comes to us through the infusion and working of the Holy Spirit, he resists the Holy Spirit himself who says through Solomon, "The will is prepared by the Lord" (Prov. 8:35, LXX), and the salutary word of the Apostle, "For God is at work in you, both to will and to work for his good pleasure" (Phil. 2:13).

CANON 5. If anyone says that not only the increase of faith but also its beginning and the very desire for faith, by which we believe in Him who justifies the ungodly and comes to the regeneration of holy baptism -- if anyone says that this belongs to us by nature and not by a gift of grace, that is, by the inspiration of the Holy

Spirit amending our will and turning it from unbelief to faith and from godlessness to godliness, it is proof that he is opposed to the teaching of the Apostles, for blessed Paul says, "And I am sure that he who began a good work in you will bring it to completion at the day of Jesus Christ" (Phil. 1:6). And again, "For by grace you have been saved through faith; and this is not your own doing, it is the gift of God" (Eph. 2:8). For those who state that the faith by which we believe in God is natural make all who are separated from the Church of Christ by definition in some measure believers.

CANON 6. If anyone says that God has mercy upon us when, apart from his grace, we believe, will, desire, strive, labor, pray, watch, study, seek, ask, or knock, but does not confess that it is by the infusion and inspiration of the Holy Spirit within us that we have the faith, the will, or the strength to do all these things as we ought; or if anyone makes the assistance of grace depend on the humility or obedience of man and does not agree that it is a gift of grace itself that we are obedient and humble, he contradicts the Apostle who says, "What have you that you did not receive?" (1 Cor. 4:7), and, "But by the grace of God I am what I am" (1 Cor. 15:10).

CANON 7. If anyone affirms that we can form any right opinion or make any right choice which relates to the salvation of eternal life, as is expedient for us, or that we can be saved, that is, assent to the preaching of the gospel through our natural powers without the illumination and inspiration of the Holy Spirit, who makes all

Appendix B: Council of Orange

men gladly assent to and believe in the truth, he is led astray by a heretical spirit, and does not understand the voice of God who says in the Gospel, "For apart from me you can do nothing" (John 15:5), and the word of the Apostle, "Not that we are competent of ourselves to claim anything as coming from us; our competence is from God" (2 Cor. 3:5).

CANON 8. If anyone maintains that some are able to come to the grace of baptism by mercy but others through free will, which has manifestly been corrupted in all those who have been born after the transgression of the first man, it is proof that he has no place in the true faith. For he denies that the free will of all men has been weakened through the sin of the first man, or at least holds that it has been affected in such a way that they have still the ability to seek the mystery of eternal salvation by themselves without the revelation of God. The Lord himself shows how contradictory this is by declaring that no one is able to come to him "unless the Father who sent me draws him" (John 6:44), as he also says to Peter, "Blessed are you, Simon Bar-Jona! For flesh and blood has not revealed this to you, but my Father who is in heaven" (Matt. 16:17), and as the Apostle says, "No one can say 'Jesus is Lord' except by the Holy Spirit" (1 Cor. 12:3).

For further reading, see also: The Council of Orange An Underrated Statement on Grace by Bradley Green, from Credo Magazine, Vol. 11, issue 2.[3]

Appendix C: Arminian Articles of 1610

Adapted from Phillip Schaff, *The Creeds of Christendom (PD)*, Volume 3, p. 546-549. My adaptation of this edition only changes the Article Headings (e.g. Article III to Article 3), and some formatting for accessibility.

Appendix C: Arminian Articles of 1610

ARTICLE 1. That God, by an eternal, unchangeable purpose in Jesus Christ his Son, before the foundation of the world, hath determined, out of the fallen, sinful race of men, to save in Christ, for Christ's sake, and through Christ, those who, through the grace of the Holy Ghost, shall believe on this his Son Jesus, and shall persevere in this faith and obedience of faith, through this grace, even to the end; and, on the other hand, to leave the incorrigible and unbelieving in sin and under wrath, and to condemn them as alienate from Christ, according to the word of the gospel in John iii. 36: 'He that believeth on the Son hath everlasting life: and he that believeth not the Son shall not see life; but the wrath of God abideth on him,' and according to other passages of Scripture also.

ARTICLE 2. That, agreeably thereto, Jesus Christ, the Saviour of the world, died for all men and for every man, so that he has obtained for them all, by his death on the cross, redemption and the forgiveness of sins; yet that no one actually enjoys this forgiveness of sins except the believer, according to the word of the Gospel of John iii. 16: 'God so loved the world that he gave his only-begotten Son, that whosoever believeth in him should not perish, but have everlasting life.' And in the First Epistle of John ii. 2: 'And he is the propitiation for our sins; and not for ours only, but also for the sins of the whole world.'

ARTICLE 3. That man has not saving grace of himself, nor of the energy of his free will, inasmuch as he, in the state of apostasy and sin, can of and by himself neither think, will, nor do any thing that is truly good (such as saving

Faith eminently is); but that it is needful that he be born again of God in Christ, through his Holy Spirit, and renewed in understanding, inclination, or will, and all his powers, in order that he may rightly understand, think, will, and effect what is truly good, according to the Word of Christ, John xv. 5: 'Without me ye can do nothing.'

ARTICLE 4. That this grace of God is the beginning, continuance, and accomplishment of all good, even to this extent, that the regenerate man himself, without prevenient or assisting, awakening, following and cooperative grace, can neither think, will, nor do good, nor withstand any temptations to evil; so that all good deeds or movements, that can be conceived, must be ascribed to the grace of God in Christ. But as respects the mode of the operation of this grace, it is not irresistible, inasmuch as it is written concerning many, that they have resisted the Holy Ghost. Acts vii., and elsewhere in many places.

ARTICLE 5. That those who are incorporated into Christ by a true faith, and have thereby become partakers of his life-giving Spirit, have thereby full power to strive against Satan, sin, the world, and their own flesh, and to win the victory; it being well understood that it is ever through the assisting grace of the Holy Ghost; and that Jesus Christ assists them through his Spirit in all temptations, extends to them his hand, and if only they are ready for the conflict, and desire his help, and are not inactive, keeps them from falling, so that they, by no craft or power of Satan, can be misled nor plucked out of Christ's hands, according to the Word of Christ, John x. 28: 'Neither shall any man pluck them out of my hand.' But whether they are capable, through negligence, of forsaking again the first beginnings of their life in Christ, of again returning to this present evil world, of turning away from the holy doctrine which was delivered them, of losing a good conscience, of becoming devoid of grace, that must be more particularly determined out of the Holy Scripture, before we ourselves can teach it with the full persuasion of our minds.

These Articles, thus set forth and taught, the Remonstrants deem agreeable to the Word of God, tending to edification, and, as regards this argument, sufficient for salvation, so that it is not necessary or edifying to rise higher or to descend deeper.

Appendix D: The Canons of Dort

Adapted from Phillip Schaff, *The Creeds of Christendom (PD)*, Volume 3, p. 582-598.

This edition adapted from Schaff omits the "rejection of errors" sections under each head of doctrine and the sentence against the Remonstrance. The unabridged version can be found in Creeds, Confessions, and Catechisms ed. Chad Van Dixhoorn, by Crossway.

My adaptation of this edition only changes the Article Headings (e.g. Article III to Article 3), removal of cross references to other sections of Schaff's volume, and some formatting for accessibility.

Appendix D: The Canons of Dort

FIRST HEAD OF DOCTRINE.

OF DIVINE PREDESTINATION.

ARTICLE 1. As all men have sinned in Adam, lie under the curse, and are obnoxious to eternal death, God would have done no injustice by leaving them all to perish, and delivering them over to condemnation on account of sin, according to the words of the Apostle (Rom. iii. 19), 'that every mouth may be stopped, and all the world may become guilty before God;' (ver. 23) 'for all have sinned, and come short of the glory of God;' and (vi. 23), 'for the wages of sin is death.'

ARTICLE 2. But 'in this the love of God was manifested, that he sent his only-begotten Son into the world,' 'that whosoever believeth on him should not perish, but have everlasting life' (1 John iv. 9; John iii. 16).

ARTICLE 3. And that men may be brought to believe, God mercifully sends the messengers of these most joyful tidings to whom he will, and at what time he pleaseth; by whose ministry men are called to repentance and faith in Christ crucified. 'How then shall they call on him in whom they have not believed? And how shall they believe in him of whom they have not heard? And how shall they hear without a preacher? And how shall they preach, except they be sent?' (Rom. x. 14, 15).

ARTICLE 4. The wrath of God abideth upon those who believe not this gospel; but such as receive it, and embrace

Jesus the Saviour by a true and living faith, are by him delivered from the wrath of God and from destruction, and have the gift of eternal life conferred upon them.

ARTICLE 5. The cause or guilt of this unbelief, as well as of all other sins, is nowise in God, but in man himself: whereas faith in Jesus Christ, and salvation through him is the free gift of God, as it is written, 'By grace ye are saved through faith, and that not of yourselves: it is the gift of God' (Eph. ii. 8); and, 'Unto you it is given in the behalf of Christ, not only to believe on him,' etc. (Phil. i. 29).

ARTICLE 6. That some receive the gift of faith from God, and others do not receive it, proceeds from God's eternal decree. 'For known unto God are all his works from the beginning of the world' (Acts xv. 18; Eph. i. 11). According to which decree he graciously softens the hearts of the elect, however obstinate, and inclines them to believe; while he leaves the non-elect in his just judgment to their own wickedness and obduracy. And herein is especially displayed the profound, the merciful, and at the same time the righteous discrimination between men, equally involved in ruin; or that decree of *election* and *reprobation*, revealed in the Word of God, which, though men of perverse, impure, and unstable minds wrest it to their own destruction, yet to holy and pious souls affords unspeakable consolation.

ARTICLE 7. Election is the unchangeable purpose of God, whereby, before the foundation of the world, he hath, out of mere grace, according to the sovereign good pleasure of his own will, chosen, from the whole human race, which had fallen through their own fault, from their primitive state of rectitude, into sin and destruction, a certain number of persons to redemption in Christ, whom he from eternity appointed the Mediator and head of the elect, and the foundation of salvation.

This elect number, though by nature neither better nor more deserving than others, but with them involved in one common misery, God hath decreed to give to Christ to be saved by him, and effectually to call and draw them to his communion by his Word and Spirit; to bestow upon them true faith, justification, and sanctification; and having powerfully preserved them in the fellowship of his Son, finally to glorify them for the demonstration of his mercy, and for the praise of the riches of his glorious grace: as it is written, 'According as he hath chosen us in him before the foundation of the world, that we should be holy and without blame before him in love; having predestinated us unto the adoption of children by Jesus Christ to himself, according to the good pleasure of his will, to the praise of the glory of his grace wherein he hath made us accepted in the Beloved' (Eph. i. 4–6). And elsewhere, 'Whom he did predestinate, them he also called; and whom he called, them he also justified; and whom he justified, them he also glorified' (Rom. viii. 30).

ARTICLE 8. There are not various decrees of election, but one and the same decree respecting all those who shall be saved both under the Old and New Testament; since the

Scripture declares the good pleasure, purpose, and counsel of the divine will to be one, according to which he hath chosen us from eternity, both to grace and to glory, to salvation and the way of salvation, which he hath ordained that we should walk therein.

ARTICLE 9. This election was not founded upon foreseen faith, and the obedience of faith, holiness, or any other good quality or disposition in man, as the prerequisite, cause, or condition on which it depended; but men are chosen to faith and to the obedience of faith, holiness, etc. Therefore election is the fountain of every saving good; from which proceed faith, holiness, and the other gifts of salvation, and finally eternal life itself, as its fruits and effects, according to that of the Apostle. 'He hath chosen us [not because we were, but] that we should be holy and without blame before him in love' (Eph. i. 4).

ARTICLE 10. The good pleasure of God is the sole cause of this gracious election; which doth not consist herein that God, foreseeing all possible qualities of human actions, elected certain of these as a condition of salvation, but that he was pleased out of the common mass of sinners to adopt some certain persons as a peculiar people to himself, as it is written, 'For the children being not yet born, neither having done any good or evil,' etc., 'it was said [namely, to Rebecca] the elder shall serve the younger; as it is written, Jacob have I loved, but Esau have I hated' (Rom. ix. 11–13); and, 'As many as were ordained to eternal life believed' (Acts xiii. 48).

ARTICLE 11. And as God himself is most wise, unchangeable, omniscient, and omnipotent, so the election made by him can neither be interrupted nor changed, recalled nor annulled; neither can the elect be cast away, nor their number diminished.

ARTICLE 12. The elect, in due time, though in various degrees and in different measures, attain the assurance of this their eternal and unchangeable election, not by inquisitively prying into the secret and deep things of God, but by observing in themselves, with a spiritual joy and holy pleasure, the infallible fruits of election pointed out in the Word of God; such as a true faith in Christ, filial fear, a godly sorrow for sin, a hungering and thirsting after righteousness, etc.

ARTICLE 13. The sense and certainty of this election afford to the children of God additional matter for daily humiliation before him, for adoring the depth of his mercies, and rendering grateful returns of ardent love to him who first manifested so great love towards them. The consideration of this doctrine of election is so far from encouraging remissness in the observance of the divine commands or from sinking men into carnal security, that these, in the just judgment of God, are the usual effects of rash presumption or of idle and wanton trifling with the grace of election, in those who refuse to walk in the ways of the elect.

ARTICLE 14. As the doctrine of divine election by the most wise counsel of God was declared by the Prophets, by

Christ himself, and by the Apostles, and is clearly revealed in the Scriptures both of the Old and New Testament, so it is still to be published in due time and place in the Church of God, for which it was peculiarly designed, provided it be done with reverence, in the spirit of discretion and piety, for the glory of God's most holy name, and for enlivening and comforting his people, without vainly attempting to investigate the secret ways of the Most High.

ARTICLE 15. What peculiarly tends to illustrate and recommend to us the eternal and unmerited grace of election is the express testimony of sacred Scripture, that not all, but some only, are elected, while others are passed by in the eternal decree; whom God, out of his sovereign, most just, irreprehensible and unchangeable good pleasure, hath decreed to leave in the common misery into which they have willfully plunged themselves, and not to bestow upon them saving faith and the grace of conversion; but permitting them in his just judgment to follow their own way; at last, for the declaration of his justice, to condemn and punish them forever, not only on account of their unbelief, but also for all their other sins. And this is the decree of reprobation which by no means makes God the author of sin (the very thought of which is blasphemy), but declares him to be an awful, irreprehensible, and righteous judge and avenger.

ARTICLE 16. Those who do not yet experience a lively faith in Christ, an assured confidence of soul, peace of conscience, an earnest endeavor after filial obedience, and glorying in God through Christ, efficaciously wrought in them, and do nevertheless persist in the use of the means which God hath appointed for working these graces in us, ought not to be alarmed at the mention of reprobation, nor to rank themselves among the reprobate, but diligently to persevere in the use of means, and with ardent desires devoutly and humbly to wait for a season of richer grace. Much less cause have they to be terrified by the doctrine of reprobation, who, though they seriously desire to be turned to God, to please him only, and to be delivered from the body of death, can not yet reach that measure of holiness and faith to which they aspire; since a merciful God has promised that he will not quench the smoking flax, nor break the bruised reed. But this doctrine is justly terrible to those who, regardless of God and of the Saviour Jesus Christ, have wholly given themselves up to the cares of the world and the pleasures of the flesh, so long as they are not seriously converted to God.

ARTICLE 17. Since we are to judge of the will of God from his Word, which testifies that the children of believers are holy, not by nature, but in virtue of the covenant of grace, in which they together with the parents are comprehended, godly parents have no reason to doubt of the election and salvation of their children whom it pleaseth God to call out of this life in their infancy.

ARTICLE 18. To those who murmur at the free grace of election, and just severity of reprobation, we answer with the Apostle: ' Nay but, O man, who art thou that repliest against God?' (Rom. ix. 20); and quote the language of our

Saviour: 'Is it not lawful for me to do what I will with mine own?' (Matt. xx. 15). And therefore with holy adoration of these mysteries, we exclaim, in the words of the Apostle: 'O the depth of the riches both of the wisdom and knowledge of God! how unsearchable are his judgments, and his ways past finding out! For who hath known the mind of the Lord, or who hath been his counselor? or who hath first given to him, and it shall be recompensed unto him again? For of him, and through him, and to him are all things: to whom be glory forever. Amen.' (Rom. xi. 33–36.)

SECOND HEAD OF DOCTRINE.

OF THE DEATH OF CHRIST, AND THE REDEMPTION OF MEN THEREBY.

ARTICLE 1. God is not only supremely merciful, but also supremely just. And his justice requires (as he hath revealed himself in his Word) that our sins committed against his infinite majesty should be punished, not only with temporal, but with eternal punishments, both in body and soul; which we can not escape, unless satisfaction be made to the justice of God.

ARTICLE 2. Since, therefore, we are unable to make that satisfaction in our own persons, or to deliver ourselves from the wrath of God, he hath been pleased of his infinite mercy to give his only-begotten Son for our surety, who was made sin, and became a curse for us and in our stead, that he might make satisfaction to divine justice on our behalf.

ARTICLE 3. The death of the Son of God is the only and most perfect sacrifice and satisfaction for sin; is of infinite worth and value, abundantly sufficient to expiate the sins of the whole world.

ARTICLE 4. This death derives its infinite value and dignity from these considerations; because the person who submitted to it was not only really man and perfectly holy, but also the only-begotten Son of God, of the same eternal and infinite essence with the Father and Holy

Spirit, which qualifications were necessary to constitute him a Saviour for us; and because it was attended with a sense of the wrath and curse of God due to us for sin.

ARTICLE 5. Moreover the promise of the gospel is, that whosoever believeth in Christ crucified shall not perish, but have everlasting life. This promise, together with the command to repent and believe, ought to be declared and published to all nations, and to all persons promiscuously and without distinction, to whom God out of his good pleasure sends the gospel.

ARTICLE 6. And, whereas many who are called by the gospel do not repent nor believe in Christ, but perish in unbelief; this is not owing to any defect or insufficiency in the sacrifice offered by Christ upon the cross, but is wholly to be imputed to themselves.

ARTICLE 7. But as many as truly believe, and are delivered and saved from sin and destruction through the death of Christ, are indebted for this benefit solely to the grace of God given them in Christ from everlasting, and not to any merit of their own.

ARTICLE 8. For this was the sovereign counsel and most gracious will and purpose of God the Father, that the quickening and saving efficacy of the most precious death of his Son should extend to all the elect, for bestowing upon them alone the gift of justifying faith, thereby to bring them infallibly to salvation: that is, it was the will of God, that Christ by the blood of the cross, whereby he confirmed the new covenant, should effectually redeem out of every people, tribe, nation, and language, all those, and those only, who were from eternity chosen to salvation, and given to him by the Father; that he should confer upon them faith, which, together with all the other saving gifts of the Holy Spirit, he purchased for them by his death; should purge them from all sin, both original and actual, whether committed before or after believing; and having faithfully preserved them even to the end, should at last bring them free from every spot and blemish to the enjoyment of glory in his own presence forever.

ARTICLE 9. This purpose proceeding from everlasting love towards the elect, has, from the beginning of the world to this day, been powerfully accomplished, and will, henceforward, still continue to be accomplished, notwithstanding all the ineffectual opposition of the gates of hell; so that the elect in due time may be gathered together into one, and that there never may be wanting a Church composed of believers, the foundation of which is laid in the blood of Christ, which may steadfastly love and faithfully serve him as their Saviour, who, as a bridegroom for his bride, laid down his life for them upon the cross; and which may celebrate his praises here and through all eternity.

Appendix D: The Canons of Dort

THIRD AND FOURTH HEADS OF DOCTRINE.

OF THE CORRUPTION OF MAN, HIS CONVERSION TO GOD, AND THE MANNER THEREOF.

ARTICLE 1. Man was originally formed after the image of God. His understanding was adorned with a true and saving knowledge of his Creator, and of spiritual things; his heart and will were upright, all his affections pure, and the whole Man was holy; but revolting from God by the instigation of the devil, and abusing the freedom of his own will, he forfeited these excellent gifts, and on the contrary entailed on himself blindness of mind, horrible darkness, vanity, and perverseness of judgment; became wicked, rebellious, and obdurate in heart and will, and impure in [all] his affections.

ARTICLE 2. Man after the fall begat children in his own likeness. A corrupt stock produced a corrupt offspring. Hence all the posterity of Adam, Christ only excepted, have derived corruption from their original parent, not by imitation, as the Pelagians of old asserted, but by the propagation of a vicious nature [in consequence of a just judgment of God].

ARTICLE 3. Therefore all men are conceived in sin, and are by nature children of wrath, incapable of any saving good, prone to evil, dead in sin, and in bondage thereto; and, without the regenerating grace of the Holy Spirit, they are neither able nor willing' to return to God, to reform the depravity of their nature, nor to dispose themselves to reformation.

ARTICLE 4. There remain, however, in man since the fall, the glimmerings of natural light, whereby he retains some knowledge of God, of natural things, and of the difference between good and evil, and discovers some regard for virtue, good order in society, and for maintaining an orderly external deportment. But so far is this light of nature from being sufficient to bring him to a saving knowledge of God, and to true conversion, that he is incapable of using it aright even in things natural and civil. Nay farther, this light, such as it is, man in various ways renders wholly polluted, and holds it [back] in unrighteousness; by doing which he becomes inexcusable before God.

ARTICLE 5. In the same light are we to consider the law of the decalogue, delivered by God to his peculiar people the Jews, by the hands of Moses. For though it discovers the greatness of sin, and more and more convinces man thereof, yet as it neither points out a remedy nor imparts strength to extricate him from misery, and thus being weak through the flesh, leaves the transgressor under the curse, man can not by this law obtain saving grace.

ARTICLE 6. What, therefore, neither the light of nature nor the law could do, that God performs by the operation of his Holy Spirit through the word or ministry of reconciliation: which is the glad tidings concerning the Messiah, by means whereof it hath pleased God to save such as believe, as well under the Old as under the New Testament.

ARTICLE 7. This mystery of his will God discovered to but a small number under the Old Testament; under the New, he reveals himself to many, without any distinction of people. The cause of this dispensation is not to be ascribed to the superior worth of one nation above another, nor to their making a better use of the light of nature, but results wholly from the sovereign good pleasure and unmerited love of God. Hence they to whom so great and so gracious a blessing is communicated, above their desert, or rather notwithstanding their demerits, are bound to acknowledge it with humble and grateful hearts, and with the Apostle to adore, not curiously to pry into the severity and justice of God's judgments displayed in others, to whom this grace is not given.

ARTICLE 8. As many as are called by the gospel are unfeignedly called; for God hath most earnestly and truly declared in his Word what will be acceptable to him, namely, that all who are called should comply with the invitation. He, moreover, seriously promises eternal life and rest to as many as shall come to him, and believe on him.

ARTICLE 9. It is not the fault of the gospel, nor of Christ offered therein, nor of God, who calls men by the gospel, and confers upon them various gifts, that those who are called by the ministry of the Word refuse to come and be converted. The fault lies in themselves; some of whom when called, regardless of their danger, reject the Word of life; others, though they receive it, suffer it not to make a lasting impression on their heart; therefore, their joy, arising only from a temporary faith, soon vanishes, and they fall away; while others choke the seed of the Word by perplexing cares and the pleasures of this world, and produce no fruit. This our Saviour teaches in the parable of the sower (Matt. xiii.).

ARTICLE 10. But that others who are called by the gospel obey the call and are converted, is not to be ascribed to the proper exercise of free-will, whereby one distinguishes himself above others equally furnished with grace sufficient for faith and conversion (as the proud heresy of Pelagius maintains); but it must be wholly ascribed to God, who, as he hath chosen his own from eternity in Christ, so he [calls them effectually in time] confers upon them faith and repentance, rescues them from the power of darkness, and translates them into the kingdom of his own Son, that they may show forth the praises of him who hath called them out of darkness into his marvelous light; and may glory not in themselves but in the Lord, according to the testimony of the Apostles in various places.

ARTICLE 11. But when God accomplishes his good pleasure in the elect, or works in them true conversion, he not only causes the gospel to be externally preached to them, and powerfully illuminates their minds by his Holy Spirit, that they may rightly understand and discern the things of the Spirit of God, but by the efficacy of the same regenerating Spirit he pervades the inmost recesses of the man; he opens the closed and softens the hardened heart, and circumcises that which was uncircumcised; infuses new qualities into the will, which, though heretofore dead, he quickens; from being evil, disobedient, and refractory, he renders it good, obedient, and pliable; actuates and strengthens it, that, like a good tree, it may bring forth the fruits of good actions.

ARTICLE 12. And this is the regeneration so highly celebrated in Scripture and denominated a new creation: a resurrection from the dead; a making alive, which God works in us without our aid. But this is nowise effected merely by the external preaching of the gospel, by moral suasion, or such a mode of operation that, after God has performed his part, it still remains in the power of man to be regenerated or not, to be converted or to continue unconverted; but it is evidently a supernatural work, most powerful, and at the same time most delightful, astonishing, mysterious, and ineffable; not inferior in efficacy to creation or the resurrection from the dead, as the Scripture inspired by the author of this work declares; so that all in whose hearts God works in this marvelous manner are certainly, infallibly, and effectually regenerated, and do actually believe. Whereupon the will thus re-newed is not only actuated and influenced by God, but, in consequence of this influence, becomes itself active. Wherefore, also, man is himself rightly said to believe and repent, by virtue of that grace received.

ARTICLE 13. The manner of this operation can not be fully comprehended by believers in this life. Notwithstanding which, they rest satisfied with knowing and experiencing that by this grace of God they are enabled to believe with the heart and to love their Saviour.

ARTICLE 14. Faith is therefore to be considered as the gift of God, not on account of its being offered by God to man, to be accepted or rejected at his pleasure, but because it is in reality conferred, breathed, and infused into him; nor even because God bestows the power or ability to believe, and then expects that man should, by the exercise of his own free will, consent to the terms of salvation, and actually believe in Christ; but because he who works in man both to will and to do, and indeed all things in all, produces both the will to believe and the act of believing also.

ARTICLE 15. God is under no obligation to confer this grace upon any; for how can he be indebted to man, who had no previous gift to bestow as a foundation for such recompense? Nay, who has nothing of his own but sin and falsehood. He, therefore, who becomes the subject of this grace owes eternal gratitude to God, and gives him thanks forever. Whoever is not made partaker thereof is either altogether regardless of these spiritual gifts and satisfied with his own condition, or is in no apprehension of danger, and vainly boasts the possession of that which he has not. With respect to those who make an external profession of faith and live regular lives, we are bound, after the example of the Apostle, to judge and speak of them in the most favorable manner; for the secret recesses of the heart are unknown to us. And as to others, who have not yet been called, it is our duty to pray for them to God, who calleth those things which be not as though they were. But we are in no wise to conduct ourselves towards them with haughtiness, as if we had made ourselves to differ.

ARTICLE 16. But as man by the fall did not cease to be a creature endowed with understanding and will, nor did sin, which pervaded the whole race of mankind, deprive him of the human nature, but brought upon him depravity and spiritual death; so also this grace of regeneration does not treat men as senseless stocks and blocks, nor take away their will and its properties, neither does violence thereto; but spiritually quickens, heals, corrects, and at the same time sweetly and powerfully bends it, that where carnal rebellion and resistance formerly prevailed a ready and sincere spiritual obedience begins to reign; in which the true and spiritual restoration and freedom of our will consist. Wherefore, unless the admirable Author of every good work wrought in us, man could have no hope of recovering from his fall by his own free will, by the abuse of which, in a state of innocence, he plunged himself into ruin.

ARTICLE 17. As the almighty operation of God, whereby he prolongs and supports this our natural life, does not exclude, but requires the use of means, by which God of his infinite mercy and goodness hath chosen to exert his influence; so also the before-mentioned supernatural operation of God, by which we are regenerated, in nowise excludes or subverts the use of the gospel, which the most wise God has ordained to be the seed of regeneration and food of the soul. Wherefore as the Apostles, and the teachers who succeeded them, piously instructed the people concerning this grace of God, to his glory and the abasement of all pride, and in the mean time, however, neglected not to keep them by the sacred precepts of the gospel, in the exercise of the Word, the sacraments and discipline; so, even to this day, be it far from either instructors or instructed to presume to tempt God in the Church by separating what he of his good pleasure hath most intimately joined together. For grace is conferred by means of admonitions; and the more readily we perform our duty, the more eminent usually is this blessing of God working in us, and the more directly is his work advanced; to whom alone all the glory, both of means and their saving fruit and efficacy, is forever due. Amen.

FIFTH HEAD OF DOCTRINE.

OF THE PERSEVERANCE OF THE SAINTS.

ARTICLE 1. Whom God calls, according to his purpose, to the communion of his Son our Lord Jesus Christ, and regenerates by the Holy Spirit, he delivers also from the dominion and slavery of sin in this life; though not altogether from the body of sin and from the infirmities of the flesh, so long as they continue in this world.

ARTICLE 2. Hence spring daily sins of infirmity, and hence spots ad-here to the best works of the saints, which furnish them with constant matter for humiliation before God, and flying for refuge to Christ crucified; for mortifying the flesh more and more by the spirit of prayer and by holy exercises of piety; and for pressing forward to the goal of perfection, till being at length delivered from this body of death, they are brought to reign with the Lamb of God in heaven.

ARTICLE 3. By reason of these remains of indwelling sin, and the temptations of sin and of the world, those who are converted could not persevere in a state of grace if left to their own strength. But God is faithful, who having conferred grace, mercifully confirms and power-fully preserves them therein, even to the end.

ARTICLE 4. Although the weakness of the flesh can not prevail against the power of God, who confirms and preserves true believers in a state of grace, yet converts are not always so influenced and actuated by the Spirit of God as not in some particular instances sinfully to deviate from the guidance of divine grace, so as to be seduced by, and to comply with, the lusts of the flesh; they must therefore be constant in watching and prayer, that they be not led into temptation. When these are neglected, they are not only liable to be drawn into great and heinous sins by Satan, the world, and the flesh, but sometimes by the righteous permission of God actually fall into these evils. This the lamentable fall of David, Peter, and other saints described in Holy Scriptures, demonstrates.

ARTICLE 5. By such enormous sins, however, they very highly offend God, incur a deadly guilt, grieve the Holy Spirit, interrupt the exercise of faith, very grievously wound their consciences, and sometimes lose the sense of God's favor, for a time, until on their returning into the right way by serious repentance, the light of God's fatherly countenance again shines upon them.

ARTICLE 6. But God, who is rich in mercy, according to his unchangeable purpose of election, does not wholly withdraw the Holy Spirit from his own people, even in their melancholy falls; nor suffer them to proceed so far as to lose the grace of adoption and forfeit the state of justification, or to commit the sin unto death;[5] nor does he permit them to be totally deserted, and to plunge themselves into everlasting destruction.

ARTICLE 7. For in the first place, in these falls he preserves in them the incorruptible seed of regeneration from perishing or being totally lost; and again, by his Word and Spirit, he certainly and effectually renews them to repentance, to a sincere and godly sorrow for their sins, that they may seek and obtain remission in the blood of the Mediator, may again experience the favor of a reconciled God, through faith adore his mercies, and henceforward more diligently work out their own salvation with fear and trembling.

ARTICLE 8. Thus, it is not in consequence of their own merits or strength, but of God's free mercy, that they do not totally fall from faith and grace, nor continue and perish finally in their backslidings; which, with respect to themselves is not only possible, but would undoubtedly happen; but with respect to God, it is utterly impossible, since his counsel can not be changed, nor his promise fail, neither can the call according to his purpose be revoked, nor the merit, intercession, and preservation of Christ be rendered ineffectual, nor the sealing of the Holy Spirit be frustrated or obliterated.

ARTICLE 9. Of this preservation of the elect to salvation, and of their perseverance in the faith, true believers for themselves may and do obtain assurance according to the measure of their faith, whereby they arrive at the certain persuasion that they ever will continue true and living members of the Church; and that they experience forgiveness of sins, and will at last inherit eternal life.

ARTICLE 10. This assurance, however, is not produced by any peculiar revelation contrary to, or independent of the

Word of God, but springs from faith in God's promises, which he has most abundantly revealed in his Word for our comfort; from the testimony of the Holy Spirit, witnessing with our spirit, that we are children and heirs of God (Rom. viii. 16); and, lastly, from a serious and holy desire to preserve a good conscience, and to perform good works. And if the elect of God were deprived of this solid comfort, that they shall finally obtain the victory, and of this infallible pledge or earnest of eternal glory, they would be of all men the most miserable.

ARTICLE 11. The Scripture moreover testifies that believers in this life have to struggle with various carnal doubts, and that under grievous temptations they are not always sensible of this full assurance of faith and certainty of persevering. But God, who is the Father of all consolation, does not suffer them to be tempted above that they are able, but will with the temptation also make a way to escape, that they may be able to bear it (1 Cor. x. 13); and by the Holy Spirit again inspires them with the comfortable assurance of persevering.

ARTICLE 12. This certainty of perseverance, however, is so far from exciting in believers a spirit of pride, or of rendering them carnally secure, that, on the contrary, it is the real source of humility, filial reverence, true piety, patience in every tribulation, fervent prayers, constancy in suffering and in confessing the truth, and of solid rejoicing in God; so that the consideration of this benefit should serve as an incentive to the serious and constant practice of gratitude and good works, as appears from the testimonies of Scripture and the examples of the saints.

ARTICLE 13. Neither does renewed confidence of persevering produce licentiousness or a disregard to piety in those who are recovered from backsliding; but it renders them much more careful and solicitous to continue in the ways of the Lord, which he hath ordained, that they who walk therein may maintain an assurance of persevering; lest by abusing his fatherly kindness, God should turn away his gracious countenance from them (to behold which is to the godly dearer than life, the withdrawing whereof is more bitter than death), and they in consequence thereof should fall into more grievous torments of conscience.

ARTICLE 14. And as it hath pleased God, by the preaching of the gospel, to begin this work of grace in us, so he preserves, continues, and perfects it by the hearing and reading of his Word, by meditation thereon, and by the exhortations, threatenings, and promises thereof, as well as by the use of the Sacraments.

ARTICLE 15. The carnal mind is unable to comprehend this doctrine of the perseverance of the saints, and the certainty thereof, which God hath most abundantly revealed in his Word, for the glory of his name and the consolation of pious souls, and which he impresses upon the hearts of the faithful. Satan abhors it; the world ridicules it; the ignorant and hypocrite abuse, and heretics oppose it. But the spouse of Christ hath always most tenderly loved and constantly defended it, as an inestimable treasure; and God, against whom neither counsel nor strength can prevail, will dispose her to continue this conduct to the end. NOW TO THIS ONE GOD, FATHER, SON, AND HOLY SPIRIT BE HONOR AND GLORY FOREVER. Amen.

CONCLUSION

And this is the perspicuous, simple, and ingenuous declaration of the orthodox doctrine respecting the five articles which have been controverted in the Belgic Churches; and the rejection of the errors, with which they have for some time been troubled. This doctrine the Synod judges to be drawn from the Word of God, and to be agreeable to the confession of the Reformed Churches. Whence it clearly appears that some, whom such conduct by no means became, have violated all truth, equity, and charity, in wishing to persuade the public:

'That the doctrine of the Reformed Churches concerning predestination, and the points annexed to it, by its own genius and. necessary tendency, leads off the minds of men from all piety and religion; that it is an opiate administered by the flesh and the devil; and the stronghold of Satan, where he lies in wait for all, and from which he wounds multitudes, and mortally strikes through many with the darts both of despair and security; that it makes God the author of sin, unjust, tyrannical, hypocritical; that it is nothing more than an interpolated Stoicism, Manicheism, Libertinism, Turcism; that it renders men carnally secure, since they are persuaded by it that nothing can hinder the salvation of the elect, let them live as they please; and, therefore, that they may safely perpetrate every species of the most atrocious crimes; and that, if the reprobate should even perform truly all the works of the saints, their obedience would not in the least contribute to their salvation; that the same doctrine teaches that God, by a mere arbitrary act of his will, without the least respect or view to any sin, has predestinated the greatest part of the world to eternal damnation, and has created them for this very purpose; that in the same manner in which the election is the fountain and cause of faith and good works, reprobation is the cause of unbelief and impiety; that many children of the faithful are torn, guiltless, from their mothers' breasts, and tyrannically plunged into hell; so that neither baptism nor the prayers of the Church at their baptism can at all profit them;' and many other things of the same kind which the Reformed Churches not only do not acknowledge, but even detest with their whole soul.

Wherefore, this Synod of Dort, in the name of the Lord, conjures as many as piously call upon the name of our Saviour Jesus Christ to judge of the faith of the Reformed Churches, not from the calumnies which on every side are heaped upon it, nor from the private expressions of a few among ancient and modern teachers, often dishonestly quoted, or corrupted and wrested to a meaning quite foreign to their intention; but from the public confessions of the Churches themselves, and from this declaration of the orthodox doctrine, confirmed by the unanimous consent of all and each of the members of the whole Synod. Moreover, the Synod warns calumniators themselves to consider the terrible judgment of God which awaits them, for bearing false witness against the confessions of so many Churches; for distressing the consciences of the weak; and for laboring to render suspected the society of the truly faithful.

Finally, this Synod exhorts all their brethren in the gospel of Christ to conduct themselves piously and religiously in handling this doctrine, both in the universities and churches; to direct it, as well in discourse as in writing, to the glory of the Divine name, to holiness of life, and to the consolation of afflicted souls; to regulate, by the Scripture, according to the analogy of faith, not only their sentiments, but also their language, and to abstain from all those phrases which exceed the limits necessary to be observed in ascertaining the genuine sense of the Holy Scriptures, and may furnish insolent sophists with a just pretext for violently assailing, or even vilifying, the doctrine of the Reformed Churches.

May Jesus Christ, the Son of God, who, seated at the Father's right hand, gives gifts to men, sanctify us in the truth; bring to the truth those who err; shut the mouths of the calumniators of sound doctrine, and endue the faithful ministers of his Word with the spirit of wisdom and discretion, that all their discourses may tend to the glory of God, and the edification of those who hear them. Amen.

Appendix E: Additional Resources

These are some additional resources on Calvinism and Arminianism for those who wish to continue their study. You will note that some of them go together (such as *Why I am Not A Calvinist* and *Why I am Not an Arminian*), which are good for comparing and contrasting the two positions in similar formats. I have put the more accessible works toward the top of each list.

FOR CALVINISM:

- 40 Questions about Calvinism by Shawn Wright
- Why I Am Not an Arminian by Peterson and Williams
- For Calvinism by Michael Horton
- Chosen by God by R.C. Sproul
- What is Reformed Theology by R.C. Sproul
- The History and Theology of Calvinism by Curt Daniel
- The Potter's Freedom by James White

Appendix E: Additional Resources

- The Five Points of Calvinism by Steele, Thomas, and Quinn
- The Reformed Doctrine of Predestination by Boettner
- The Doctrines of Grace James Boice
- Redemption Accomplished and Applied by John Murray
- The Canons of Dort and Reformed Confessions can be accessed in Crossway's Publications of Creeds, Confessions, and Catechisms ed., Chad Van Dixhoorn
- Monergism.com is a free online theological library comprised of Reformed Christian resources on many topics.

FOR ARMINIANISM:

- 40 Questions about Arminianism by Matthew Pinson
- Why I Am Not a Calvinist by Walls and Dongell
- Against Calvinism by Roger Olson
- Grace, Faith, Free Will by Robert Picirilli
- Classical Arminianism by Leroy Forlines
- Arminian Theology: Myths and Realities by Roger Olson
- The Transforming Power of Grace by Thomas Oden
- Grace for All: The Arminian Dynamics of Salvation by Clark Pinnock
- Jacob Arminius: Theologian of Grace by Keith Stranglin

Appendix E: Additional Resources

- Prevenient Grace by Brian Shelton
- Whosoever Will by David Allen
- evangelicalarminians.org is the website of the Society of Evangelical Arminians (SEA). The SEA is an association of evangelical scholars and laymen who adhere to Arminian theology and their website promotes and advances Arminian theology.

BOTH [OR MORE] PERSPECTIVES:

- Predestination and Free Will: Four Views of Divine Sovereignty and Human Freedom, ed. Basinger & Basinger
- Divine Foreknowledge: Four Views, ed. Beilby
- Four Views on Divine Providence, ed. Jowers & Gundry
- Four Views on Eternal Security, ed. Pinson
- Debating Calvinism by Hunt and White

Notes

Introduction

1. The term is being used in its more inclusive "three Cs" sense. See Appendix A.

1. Historical Points of Interest

1. The doctrines concerning the person and work of Christ.
2. Robert Peterson and Michael Williams, *Why I Am Not Arminian* (Downers Grove, IL: InterVarsity Press, 2004), p. 36.
3. 5th Century being AD 401-500
4. A scholar who is particularly challenging the traditional view is Ali Bonner via her work, The Myth of Pelagianism. While some have taken her position, other scholars, such as Daniel James Watson, Stuart Squires, Josef Lössl, remain unconvinced of her thesis.
5. Catholicism would include Mary in this category.
6. Augustine, The City of God, 14.27
7. Robert Peterson and Michael Williams, *Why I Am Not Arminian* (Downers Grove, IL: InterVarsity Press, 2004), p. 24.
8. Ibid.
9. Ibid, 30.
10. In Lutheranism baptismal regeneration is still seen as passively receiving God's grace.
11. Matthew Pinson, *40 Questions About Arminianism* (Grand Rapids, MI: Kregel Academic: Kregel Publications , 2022), p. 212.
12. Ibid, 213.
13. Ibid.
14. Ibid, 215.
15. Ibid, 216.
16. Daniel, Curt. The History and Theology of Calvinism, p 14.
17. Orton Wiley, *Christian Theology*, vol. 2, 3 vols. (Beacon Hill Press, 1952), 2:103.
18. Peterson, Robert; Williams, Michael. Why I am Not an Arminian, p. 36.

Notes

19. Ibid, 37.
20. Herman Bavinck, *Reformed Dogmatics: Abridged*, ed. John Bolt (Grand Rapids, MI: Baker Academic, n.d.), 38-39.
21. Roger Olson, *Arminian Theology: Myths and Realities* (Downers Grove, IL: InterVarsity Press, 2006), p. 81.
22. Robert Peterson and Michael Williams, *Why I Am Not Arminian* (Downers Grove, IL: InterVarsity Press, 2004), p. 38.
23. Roger Olson is emphatic on this in his Arminian Theology Myths and Realities.
24. Peterson and Williams for example, ibid, 39.
25. Robert Godfrey, *Saving the Reformation: The Pastoral Theology of the Canons of Dort* (Sanford, FL: Ligonier Ministries, 2019), p. 2.
26. Ibid, 17.
27. Nick Needham, *2000 Years of Christ's Power*, vol. 3 (London: Grace Publications Truth, 2016), p. 88.
28. Charles Cortright, "Luther and Erasmus: The Debate on the Freedom of the Will," [*Arizona-California District Pastoral Conference, October 25-27, 1988, Mt. Olive Ev. Lutheran Church, Las Vegas, Nevada*, n.d.
29. Nick Needham, *2000 Years of Christ's Power*, vol. 3 (London: Grace Publications Truth, 2016), p. 137.
30. Ibid.
31. Robert Peterson and Michael Williams, *Why I Am Not Arminian* (Downers Grove, IL: InterVarsity Press, 2004), p. 93.
32. Ibid.
33. Ibid, 99.
34. Ibid, 116.
35. Ibid.

2. Total Depravity

1. David Allen and Steve Lemke, eds., *Calvinism: A Biblical and Theological Critique* (Nashville, TN: B&H Academic, 3033), pp. 37-38). Kindle Edition.
2. Gerald Bray, "Original Sin in Patristic Thought," Churchman 108, no. 1 (1994): 37, found in Harwood's contribution of Calvinism: A Biblical and Theological Critique
3. Ibid, 46.
4. Stanley J. Grenz, David Guretzki, and Cherith Fee Nordling, eds., *Pocket Theological Terms*, Accordance electronic, Pocket Dictionary of Theological Terms (Downers Grove: InterVarsity Press, 1999), ent. Imputation.

Notes

5. David S. Dockery, *Holman Illustrated Bible Dictionary*, s.v. "IMPUTE, IMPUTATION," Accordance ed. paragraph 8484.
6. Ibid.
7. John Harvey, *Romans*, ed. Andreas J. Köstenberger and Robert Yarbrough, Exegetical Guide to the Greek New Testament (Nashville, TN: B&H Academic, 2017)., p. 138.
8. Douglas J. Moo, *Romans*, ed. D. A Carson et al., Accordance electronic, New Bible Commentary: 21st Century Edition (Downers Grove: Inter-Varsity Press, 1994), p.350.
9. Ibid.
10. Ibid.
11. Curt Daniel, *The History and Theology of Calvinism* (Darlington, CO: EP Books, 2019), 284.
12. Douglas J. Moo, *Romans*, ed. D. A Carson et al., Accordance electronic, New Bible Commentary: 21st Century Edition (Downers Grove: Inter-Varsity Press, 1994), p. 354.
13. Michael Patton, "Are We Really Held Guilty for the Sin of Another?," n.d., https://credohouse.org/blog/are-we-really-held-guilty-for-the-sin-of-another
14. The particular baptists are those Calvinistic baptists differing from the General or "free-will baptists."
15. The Great Exchange, https://www.ligonier.org/learn/devotionals/great-exchange
16. Matthew Pinson, *40 Questions About Arminianism* (Grand Rapids, MI: Kregel Academic: Kregel Publications , 2022), p. 208.
17. Ibid.
18. Disputations, 152-153.
19. Ibid.
20. Arminius, Disputations of Some of the Principle Subjects of the Christian Religion, Works, 256, found in Pinson.
21. Leroy Forlines, *Classical Arminianism* (Nashville, TN: Randall House Publications, 2011), 26.
22. Ibid, 32-33.
23. *Pocket Dictionary of Theological Terms*, s.v. "depravity, total depravity," 37.
24. Curt Daniels, The History and Theology of Calvinism, 289.
25. Ibid, 289.
26. Ibid.
27. Ibid, 290.
28. Minding the Heart, by Robert Saucy as an excellent resource on the heart in Hebraic thought and in sanctification.

Notes

29. Douglas J. Moo, *Romans*, ed. D. A Carson et al., Accordance electronic, New Bible Commentary: 21st Century Edition (Downers Grove: InterVarsity Press, 1994), p. 210.
30. Matthew Pinson, *40 Questions About Arminianism* (Grand Rapids, MI: Kregel Academic: Kregel Publications , 2022), p. 207.
31. Ibid, 208.
32. Ibid, 209.
33. Jacob Arminius, Public Disputation 11, on the Free Will of Man and Its Powers," found in Pinson.
34. Ibid.
35. Matthew Pinson, *40 Questions About Arminianism* (Grand Rapids, MI: Kregel Academic: Kregel Publications , 2022), p. 209-210.
36. Can be accessed at http://evangelicalarminians.org/the-arminian-confession-of-1621/ and "The Arminian Confession of 1621 (Princeton Theological Monograph), translated by Mark Ellis, 2005.
37. Orthodox Creed, articles 15 and 20. http://baptiststudiesonline.com/wp-content/uploads/2007/02/orthodox-creed.pdf, accessed September 17, 2020. Pulled from Pinson, J. Matthew. 40 Questions About Arminianism (p. 220).
38. Pinson, J. Matthew. 40 Questions About Arminianism (p. 220).
39. Timothy Tennent, "Prevenient Grace: Why I Am a Methodist and an Evangelical," https://timothytennent.com/prevenient-grace-why-i-am-a-methodist-and-an-evangelical-part-2/
40. Leroy Forlines, *Classical Arminianism* (Nashville, TN: Randall House Publications, 2011), 16-17.
41. Ibid, 17.
42. Ibid.
43. Ibi, 22.
44. Ibid.
45. Roger Olson, in his book Arminian Theology: Myths and Realities, counters the Calvinist idea that Arminianism is the most popular theology in the modern pulpit. He points out that pop-theology is often semi-Pelagian or full Pelagianism and that this charge is false on the grounds. Historic Arminian theology is not semi or full Pelagian. See Olson, Arminian Theology, p. 30.

3. The Human Will

1. Wiesner lists the following articles: Todd S. Beall, *Josephus' Description of the Essenes Illustrated by the Dead Sea Scrolls* (Cambridge: Cambridge University Press, 1988), 113–14; Gabriele Boccaccini, "Inner-Jewish

Notes

Debate on the Tension between Divine and Human Agency in Second-Temple Judaism," in *Divine and Human Agency in Paul and His Cultural Environment,* ed. John M. G. Barclay and Simon J. Gathercole (London: T&T Clark, 2007), 15; Jonathan Klawans, "Josephus on Fate, Free Will, and Ancient Jewish Types of Compatibilism," *Numen* 56 (2009): 44–90; Jason Maston, *Divine and Human Agency in Second Temple Judaism and Paul,* WUNT 2/297 (Tübingen: Mohr Siebeck, 2010), 10–18.

2. Klawans, Jonathan. "Josephus on Fate, Free Will, and Ancient Jewish Types of Compatibilism." *Numen* 56, no. 1 (2009): 44–90. http://www.jstor.org/stable/27643351.
3. Lee-Barnewall, Joel Green and Lee Martin McDonald, eds., *The World of the New Testament* (Grand Rapids, MI: Baker Academic, 2013), p. 221.
4. Wiesner, Robert. "Predestinarian Election in Second Temple Judaism and its relevance to Pauline theology," Historical and Theological Studies, Westminster Theological Journal 82.
5. Lee-Barnewall, Joel Green and Lee Martin McDonald, eds., *The World of the New Testament* (Grand Rapids, MI: Baker Academic, 2013), p. 221.
6. Matthew Pinson, *40 Questions About Arminianism* (Grand Rapids, MI: Kregel Academic: Kregel Publications , 2022), p. 224.
7. Ibid, 226.
8. Ibid.
9. Ibid.
10. Jerry Walls and Joseph Dongell, *Why I Am Not a Calvinist* (Downers Grove, IL: InterVarsity Press, 2004), p 103-104.
11. Roger Olson, *Arminian Theology: Myths and Realities* (Downers Grove, IL: InterVarsity Press, 2006), 71.
12. Leroy Forlines, *Classical Arminianism* (Nashville, TN: Randall House Publications, 2011), 21
13. Christensen, Scott. What about Free Will?: Reconciling Our Choices with God's Sovereignty. P&R Publishing. Kindle Edition, p. 17.
14. Olson, Arminian Theology: Myths and Realities, 98.
15. Matthew Pinson, *40 Questions About Arminianism* (Grand Rapids, MI: Kregel Academic: Kregel Publications , 2022), 230.
16. Matthew Pinson, *40 Questions About Arminianism* (Grand Rapids, MI: Kregel Academic: Kregel Publications , 2022), p. 261.
17. Ibid.
18. Ibid, 262.
19. Ibid.
20. Ibid.

Notes

21. Ibid.
22. Olson, Arminian Theology: Myths and Realities, p. 116.
23. Ibid, 117.
24. Ibid, 120.
25. Ibid, 121.
26. Ibid, 122-123.
27. Matthew Pinson, *40 Questions About Arminianism* (Grand Rapids, MI: Kregel Academic: Kregel Publications , 2022), 265.
28. Ibid, 265.
29. Ibid.
30. John Frame, *The Doctrine of God* (Phillipsberg, NJ: P&R Publishing, 2002), Kindle Locations 1698-1703, p. 136 in print.
31. Wright illustrates this same point in 40 Questions About Calvinism, 40 Questions Series, p. 76.
32. Shawn Wright, *40 Questions about Calvinism* (Grand Rapids, MI: Kregel Academic: Kregel Publications , 2019), 79.
33. Ibid.
34. Robert Peterson and Michael Williams, *Why I Am Not Arminian* (Downers Grove, IL: InterVarsity Press, 2004), p. 142.
35. Ibid, 143.
36. Ibid, 144.
37. Ibid, 146.
38. Renihan, James. *To the Judicious and Impartial Reader: An Exposition on the 1689 London Baptist Confession of Faith*. Vol. 2. 2 vols. Baptist Symbolics. Cape Coral, FL: Founders Press, 2022, 154.
39. Compare the description of Jacob Arminius from Olson, quoted when discussing Arminians and Sovereignty.
40. Scott Christensen, *What About Free Will? Reconciling Our Choices with God's Sovereignty* (Phillipsberg, NJ: P&R Publishing, 2016), pp. 45-46. Kindle Edition.
41. Ibid, 44
42. Wright, Shawn D.. 40 Questions About Calvinism (40 Questions Series) (p. 90). Kregel Academic: Kregel Publications & Professional. Kindle Edition.
43. Robert Peterson and Michael Williams, *Why I Am Not Arminian* (Downers Grove, IL: InterVarsity Press, 2004), p. 151.
44. Scott Christensen, *What About Free Will? Reconciling Our Choices with God's Sovereignty* (Phillipsberg, NJ: P&R Publishing, 2016), p. 106. Kindle Edition.
45. Ibid.
46. Curt Daniel, *The History and Theology of Calvinism* (Darlington, CO: EP Books, 2019), p.215.

Notes

4. The Doctrine of Grace

1. Matthew Pinson, *40 Questions About Arminianism* (Grand Rapids, MI: Kregel Academic: Kregel Publications , 2022), p. 282.
2. Ibid, 283.
3. Brian Abasciano, The FACTS of Salvation: A Summary of Arminian Theology/the Biblical Doctrines of Grace, http://evangelicalarminians.org/the-facts-of-salvation-a-summary-of-arminian-theologythe-biblical-doctrines-of-grace/
4. Ibid.
5. Ibid.
6. Ibid.
7. Matthew Pinson, *40 Questions About Arminianism* (Grand Rapids, MI: Kregel Academic: Kregel Publications , 2022), p. 284
8. Ibid.
9. Ibid.
10. Stephen Ashby, "A Reformed Arminian Response to J. Steven Harper," in Four Views on Eternal Security, 273. Found in Pinson, 40 Questions About Arminianism, 286-287.
11. Matthew Pinson, *40 Questions About Arminianism* (Grand Rapids, MI: Kregel Academic: Kregel Publications , 2022), p. 287.
12. Ibid, 288.
13. Ibid, 322.
14. Ibid, 337-338.
15. Ibid.
16. Ibid, 340.
17. Shawn Wright, *40 Questions about Calvinism* (Grand Rapids, MI: Kregel Academic: Kregel Publications, 2019), 207.
18. Ibid, 214.
19. 2LBCF, 10.4 see also WCF 10.4
20. Bruce Demarest, *The Cross and Salvation: The Doctrine of Salvation* (Wheaton, IL: Crossway, 1997), 222.
21. Ibid.
22. Ibid.
23. Thomas R. Schreiner, "Does Scripture Teach Prevenient Grace in the Wesleyan Sense?," in The Grace of God, the Bondage of the Will, Vol. 2: Historical and Theological Perspectives on Calvinism, ed. Thomas R. Schreiner and Bruce A. Ware (Grand Rapids: Baker, 1995), 376.
24. Ibid.
25. Murray Harris, *John*, Exegetical Guide to the Greek New Testament (Nashville, TN: B&H Publishing, 2015), p. 234.
26. J. Ramsey Michaels, *The gospel of John*, New International Commen-

tary on the New Testament. Accordance electronic ed. (Grand Rapids: Eerdmans, 2010), 699-700.
27. Ibid, 700-701.
28. Sam Storms, the Arminian Doctrine of Prevenient Grace, from https://www.samstorms.org/all-articles/post/the-arminian-doctrine-of-prevenient-grace
29. Shawn Wright, 40 Questions about Calvinism, p. 251.
30. Ibid.
31. Ibid.
32. Ibid, 252.
33. Ibid.
34. Ibid.
35. Ibid.
36. Ibid.
37. Ibid, 256.

5. Conversion and Regeneration

1. Bruce Demarest, *The Cross and Salvation: The Doctrine of Salvation* (Wheaton, IL: Crossway, 1997), 264-265.
2. R.C. Sproul, *Chosen by God* (Carol Stream, IL: Tyndale House Publishers, 1986), 72
3. Shawn Wright, *40 Questions about Calvinism* (Grand Rapids, MI: Kregel Academic: Kregel Publications, 2019), p. 217.
4. Thomas R. Schreiner, "Does Regeneration Necessarily Precede Conversion?" https://9marks.org/article/does-regeneration-necessarily-precede-conversion/.
5. Matt Slick, https://carm.org/about-theology/does-regeneration-precede-faith-or-does-faith-precede-regeneration/
6. Ibid.
7. Louis Berkhof, *Systematic Theology* (Louisville, KY: GLH Publishing, 2017), 536
8. Leroy Forlines, *Classical Arminianism* (Nashville, TN: Randall House Publications, 2011), p 86.

6. Predestination and Election

1. Stanley J. Grenz, David Guretzki, and Cherith Fee Nordling, eds., *Pocket Theological Terms*, Accordance electronic, Pocket Dictionary of

Notes

Theological Terms (Downers Grove: InterVarsity Press, 1999) "election," 43-44.
2. Timothy George, *Holman Illustrated Bible Dictionary*, s.v. "ELECTION," paragraph 5067.
3. Ibid.
4. Ibid, para. 5070.
5. Ibid.
6. Chad Brand, *Holman Illustrated Bible Dictionary*, s.v. "PREDESTINATION," paragraph 13843.
7. Matthew Pinson, *40 Questions About Arminianism* (Grand Rapids, MI: Kregel Academic: Kregel Publications , 2022), p. 411.
8. Roger Olson, *Arminian Theology: Myths and Realities* (Downers Grove, IL: InterVarsity Press, 2006), 181.
9. Ibid, 180.
10. Ibid.
11. Matthew Pinson, *40 Questions About Arminianism* (Grand Rapids, MI: Kregel Academic: Kregel Publications , 2022), p. 412
12. Ibid.
13. Ibid, 413.
14. Ibid, 416.
15. Ibid, 377.
16. Ibid, 378.
17. Ibid.
18. Ibid, 382.
19. Ibid, 361.
20. Ibid, 386.
21. Ibid, 387.
22. Ibid, 390.
23. Ibid, 391.
24. Ibid.
25. Ibid.
26. Ibid, 392.
27. Ibid, 393.
28. Ibid, 394.
29. Ibid, 395.
30. Ibid, 395-396.
31. Ibid.
32. Ibid.
33. Ibid.
34. Ibid, 395-396.
35. Shawn Wright, *40 Questions about Calvinism* (Grand Rapids, MI: Kregel Academic: Kregel Publications, 2019), 158.

Notes

36. Ibid.
37. Ibid, 159.
38. Douglas J. Moo, *Romans*, ed. D. A Carson et al., Accordance electronic, New Bible Commentary: 21st Century Edition (Downers Grove: Inter-Varsity Press, 1994), p. 553-554.
39. John Harvey, *Romans*, ed. Andreas J. Köstenberger and Robert Yarbrough, Exegetical Guide to the Greek New Testament (Nashville, TN: B&H Academic, 2017), 210.
40. Shawn Wright, 40 Questions About Calvinism, 158.
41. Deffinbaugh, B. (2004, May 18). 10. The Sovereignty of God in Salvation - (Romans 9:1-24). Retrieved from https://bible.org/series-page/sovereignty-god-salvation-romans-91-24
42. Harvey, J. D. (2017). *Exegetical Guide to the Greek: Romans*. Nashville, TN: B&H Academic, 231.
43. The best discussion on the subject that is accessible is Predestinarian Election in Second Temple Judaism and its relevance to Pauline Theology by Robert Wiesner in the WTJ, 82, 2020, 17-32.
44. Predestinarian Election in Second Temple Judaism and its relevance to Pauline Theology by Robert Wiesner in the WTJ, 82, 2020, 17-32.
45. Cited from The New Oxford Annotated Apocrypha, Fifth Edition, Oxford University Press, New York, New York, 2018.
46. Predestinarian Election in Second Temple Judaism and its relevance to Pauline Theology by Robert Wiesner in the WTJ, 82, 2020, 17-32.
47. Ibid.
48. Predestinarian Election in Second Temple Judaism and its relevance to Pauline Theology by Robert Wiesner in the WTJ, 82, 2020, 17-32.

7. The Atonement: its Extent and Otherwise

1. Matthew Pinson, *40 Questions About Arminianism* (Grand Rapids, MI: Kregel Academic: Kregel Publications , 2022), p. 125.
2. Curt Daniel, *The History and Theology of Calvinism* (Darlington, CO: EP Books, 2019), p 493.
3. Philip Schaff, *The Creeds of Christendom*, Vol. 3, Bibliotheca symbolica ecclesiae universalis (New York: Harper Longmans, 1919), 587.
4. Ibid, 587.
5. John Calvin, *Calvin's Commentaries (Complete)*, trans. John King, Accordance electronic ed. (Edinburgh: Calvin Translation Society, 1847), paragraph 88415.
6. Ibid. on Colossians, paragraph 90886
7. Daniel, Curt. The History and Theology of Calvinism, p 493.

8. Ibid.

8. Perseverance of the Saints

1. Herman Bavinck, *Reformed Dogmatics: Abridged*, ed. John Bolt (Grand Rapids, MI: Baker Academic, n.d.), 584.
2. Ibid.
3. Philip Schaff, *The Creeds of Christendom*, Vol. 3. Bibliotheca symbolica ecclesiae universalis. (New York: Harper Longmans, 1919), 637.
4. Ibid, 411.
5. Louis Berkhof, *Systematic Theology* (Louisville, KY: GLH Publishing, 2017), 548
6. Herman Bavinck, *Reformed Dogmatics : Volume 4: Holy Spirit, Church, and New Creation*, ed. John Bolt, vol. 4, 4 vols. (Grand Rapids, MI: Baker Academic, 2008), 267-68
7. Shawn Wright, *40 Questions about Calvinism* (Grand Rapids, MI: Kregel Academic: Kregel Publications, 2019), 227.
8. See also Appendix D, Fifth Head of Doctrine
9. Matthew Pinson, *40 Questions About Arminianism* (Grand Rapids, MI: Kregel Academic: Kregel Publications , 2022), p. 441.
10. Matthew Pinson, *40 Questions About Arminianism* (Grand Rapids, MI: Kregel Academic: Kregel Publications , 2022), p. 445
11. Ibid, 455.
12. Ibid. 516.
13. Ibid, 519-520.

Appendix A: What does "Reformed" mean?

1. "What Does it Mean to be Reformed," https://tabletalkmagazine.com/article/2018/11/what-does-it-mean-to-be-reformed/

Appendix B: Council of Orange

1. Philip Schaff, *Nicene and Post-nicene Christianity*, vol. 3 of History Of The Christian Church. Accordance electronic ed. (New York: Charles Scribner's Sons, 1910), paragraph 12791; p. 869, in print. ed. by Hendrickson Publishers Marketing.
2. Pulled from https://www.monergism.com/thethreshold/articles/

Notes

onsite/Orange5-8.html, see also the full text here: https://www.monergism.com/thethreshold/articles/onsite/councilorange.html

3. https://credomag.com/article/the-council-of-orange/

Select Bibliography

Allen, David, and Steve Lemke, eds. *Calvinism: A Biblical and Theological Critique*. Nashville, TN: B&H Academic, 3033.

Arminius, Jacob. *Disputations of Some of the Principle Subjects of the Christian Religion, from the Complete Works of Jacob Arminius*, n.d.

Augustine. *The City of God*, n.d.

Bavinck, Herman. *Reformed Dogmatics: Abridged*. Edited by John Bolt. Grand Rapids, MI: Baker Academic, n.d.

———. *Reformed Dogmatics: Volume 4: Holy Spirit, Church, and New Creation*. Edited by John Bolt. Vol. 4. 4 vols. Grand Rapids, MI: Baker Academic, 2008.

Berkhof, Louis. *Systematic Theology*. Louisville, KY: GLH Publishing, 2017.

Bray, Gerald. "Original Sin in Patristic Thought." *Churchmen* 108, no. 1 (1994).

Butler, Trent C., Chad Brand, Charles Draper, and Archie England, eds. *Holman Dictionary*. Accordance electronic. Holman Illustrated Bible Dictionary. Nashville: B&H Publishing Group, 2003.

Christensen, Scott. *What About Free Will? Reconciling Our Choices with God's Sovereignty*. Phillipsberg, NJ: P&R Publishing, 2016.

Cortright, Charles. "Luther and Erasmus: The Debate on the Freedom of the Will." [Arizona-California District Pastoral Conference, October 25-27, 1988, Mt. Olive Ev. Lutheran Church, Las Vegas, Nevada, n.d.

Daniel, Curt. *The History and Theology of Calvinism*. Darlington, CO: EP Books, 2019.

Demarest, Bruce. *The Cross and Salvation: The Doctrine of Salvation*. Wheaton, IL: Crossway, 1997.

Forlines, Leroy. *Classical Arminianism*. Nashville, TN: Randall House Publications, 2011.

Frame, John. *The Doctrine of God*. Phillipsberg, NJ: P&R Publishing, 2002.

Godfrey, Robert. *Saving the Reformation: The Pastoral Theology of the Canons of Dort*. Sanford, FL: Ligonier Ministries, 2019.

Green, Joel, and Lee Martin McDonald, eds. *The World of the New Testament*. Grand Rapids, MI: Baker Academic, 2013.

Grenz, Stanley J., David Guretzki, and Cherith Fee Nordling, eds. *Pocket*

Select Bibliography

Theological Terms. Accordance electronic. Pocket Dictionary of Theological Terms. Downers Grove: InterVarsity Press, 1999.

Harris, Murray. *John.* Exegetical Guide to the Greek New Testament. Nashville, TN: B&H Publishing, 2015.

Harvey, John. *Romans.* Edited by Andreas J. Köstenberger and Robert Yarbrough. Exegetical Guide to the Greek New Testament. Nashville, TN: B&H Academic, 2017.

Klawans, Jonathan. "Josephus on Fate, Free Will, and Ancient Jewish Types of Compatibilism" Numen, no. 1 (2009): 44–90.

Ligonier. "The Great Exchange," n.d. https://www.ligonier.org/learn/devotionals/great-exchange.

Michaels, J. Ramsey. *The Gospel of John.* Accordance electronic. New International Commentary on the New Testament. Grand Rapids: Eerdmans, 2010.

Moo, Douglas J. *Romans.* Edited by D. A Carson, R. T France, J. A. Motyer, and Gordon J. Wenham. Accordance electronic. New Bible Commentary: 21st Century Edition. Downers Grove: InterVarsity Press, 1994.

Needham, Nick. *2000 Years of Christ's Power.* Vol. 3. London: Grace Publications Truth, 2016.

Olson, Roger. *Arminian Theology: Myths and Realities.* Downers Grove, IL: InterVarsity Press, 2006.

Patton, Michael. "Are We Really Held Guilty for the Sin of Another?," n.d. https://credohouse.org/blog/are-we-really-held-guilty-for-the-sin-of-another.

Peterson, Robert, and Michael Williams. *Why I Am Not Arminian.* Downers Grove, IL: InterVarsity Press, 2004.

Pinson, Matthew. *40 Questions About Arminianism.* Grand Rapids, MI: Kregel Academic: Kregel Publications, 2022.

Renihan, James. *To the Judicious and Impartial Reader: An Exposition on the 1689 London Baptist Confession of Faith.* Vol. 2. 2 vols. Baptist Symbolics. Cape Coral, FL: Founders Press, 2022.

Saucy, Robert. *Minding the Heart.* Grand Rapids, MI: Kregel Publications, 2013.

Schreiner, Thomas. "Does Regeneration Necessarily Precede Conversion?," n.d. https://9marks.org/article/does-regeneration-necessarily-precede-conversion/.

———. *Does Scripture Teach Prevenient Grace in the Wesleyan Sense.* Vol. The Grace of God, the Bondage of the Will. Vol. 2: Historical and Theological Perspectives on Calvinism. Grand Rapids, MI: Baker Academic, 1995.

Slick, Matthew. "Does Regeneration Precede Faith or Does Faith Precede Regeneration," n.d. https://carm.org/about-theology/does-regeneration-precede-faith-or-does-faith-precede-regeneration/.

Sproul, R.C. *Chosen by God*. Carol Stream, IL: Tyndale House Publishers, 1986.

Tennent, Timothy. "Prevenient Grace: Why I Am a Methodist and an Evangelical," n.d. https://timothytennent.com/tag/grace.

"The Facts of Salvation A Summary of Arminian Theology: The Biblical Doctrines of Grace," n.d. http://evangelicalarminians.org/the-facts-of-salvation-a-summary-of-arminian-theologythe-biblical-doctrines-of-grace/.

Walls, Jerry, and Joseph Dongell. *Why I Am Not a Calvinist*. Downers Grove, IL: InterVarsity Press, 2004.

Wiesner, Robert. "Predestinarian Election in Second Temple Judaism and Its Relevance to Pauline Theology." *Westminster Theological Journal* Historical and Theological Studies, no. 82 (n.d.).

Wiley, Orton. *Christian Theology*. Vol. 2. 3 vols. Beacon Hill Press, 1952.

Wright, Shawn. *40 Questions about Calvinism*. Grand Rapids, MI: Kregel Academic Kregel Publications, 2019.

Index

A

Aaron, 145
ability, 13, 15, 47, 53–54, 56, 69, 72–73, 79, 85–86, 103, 124
Abraham, 36, 145, 159–161, 176
Adam, 5–7, 14, 20, 23, 32–37, 39–46, 55, 57, 59–60, 65, 96, 106, 112, 149
adoption, 151, 157, 168
affection, 100, 155
Anselm, 34
anthropology, 13
apology, 44
apostasy, 55, 206, 209, 211–212
apostates, 206–207
apostatize, 207, 210
apostatized, 208
apostle, 54, 166, 174, 198
Arminian, 3, 10, 15–16, 21, 24, 26, 28, 45, 47, 52–53, 60, 62, 66, 75–78, 80–82, 88, 90, 99–100, 103–104, 106–108, 110–111, 113, 116–117, 120, 124, 126–128, 134–135, 140, 143–144, 149–150, 152, 157–160, 165–166, 175, 180, 185, 191, 199, 209–212
arminianism, 1, 9–11, 17–18, 24, 27, 31, 35, 39, 44–47, 53, 56, 58, 65, 76, 78, 80–82, 88, 90, 97, 99, 101, 106, 108, 111–112, 132–137, 140–142, 149, 151–152, 154, 157, 159, 174, 187–188, 199, 201, 209, 213, 215–216
arminius, 10, 21, 23–27, 44–46, 53–55, 71, 77–79, 88, 101, 151, 154–155, 159–160, 163, 189
assurance, 146, 173, 206, 210
Assyria, 92
Assyrians, 92
atone, 190
atoned, 192
atonement, 2–3, 27, 29, 46, 101, 103, 106, 112, 121, 187–199, 201
Augustine, 3, 5–8, 13–14, 20, 34, 36–38, 68–70
Augustinian, 16–17, 19–20
Augustinianism, 17

Index

B
backsliding, 211
baptism, 3, 13
baptist, 29, 43, 60, 84, 87–88, 102, 192, 198
baptize, 198
baptized, 198
Barnabas, 166
belgic, 24–25, 44, 54, 189, 205
believer, 45, 139, 155, 173, 209, 211–212
beza, 12, 21, 23, 25
blessed, 157, 182, 216
blessing, 102

C
Calvin, 21, 29, 34, 195, 206
calvinism, 1, 11, 21–22, 29, 31, 34–35, 39–40, 43, 47–48, 59–60, 65, 82, 88, 94, 99, 111, 113, 121–123, 128, 133, 135–136, 142, 165, 169, 171, 174–175, 187–188, 194, 199, 201–202, 210, 215–216
calvinist, 15, 18, 45, 47, 53, 58–59, 66, 72, 77, 82, 84–85, 89–90, 99–100, 108–110, 113, 115–116, 118, 120–124, 127–129, 132, 134–137, 139–141, 144, 158, 165, 170–171, 174–175, 177–178, 187–188, 191, 193, 196–199, 201, 203, 205, 208
calvinistic, 29, 82, 116, 119, 206, 208
catechism, 24–25, 44, 54, 189
catholicism, 20
Colossians, 196
communion, 164, 168
compassion, 161–162, 178
compassioned, 178
compatibilism, 61, 66, 68–69, 82–83, 85–86, 90, 97, 181, 187, 205
compatibilist, 73, 83, 90, 92–94
compatibilistic, 181
compatibility, 76, 94
compatible, 66, 83
condemnation, 12, 22, 38–41, 44, 51, 57
condemned, 5–6, 12–13, 15, 40–41, 51
conditional, 25, 27, 34, 97, 142–143, 148–150, 152–153, 157–158, 161, 163–165, 174, 178, 180, 185, 209
confession, 24–25, 29, 42–44, 54–55, 60, 84, 87–88, 114, 189, 202,

Index

204–206, 208
conversion, 7, 9, 11, 13, 15, 72, 101, 103–106, 112, 114–115, 135, 137, 139, 141, 169, 208
cooperation, 7, 9–10, 13, 178
Corinthians, 38, 40, 49, 148
corruption, 3, 5–6, 14–16, 32–36, 46–48, 50–51, 54–57, 59–60, 63, 138, 204
covenant, 145, 147, 159–161, 163, 195, 204
creation, 13, 22, 32–33, 77, 86, 104, 118, 144, 148, 182–183, 196
creator, 59, 79, 118, 181
creature, 74, 87, 90, 139, 179
creaturely, 71, 74, 77, 86, 97
crucified, 33, 93
crucifixion, 93, 95
culpability, 93
culpable, 75, 89

D

damnation, 8, 16, 22, 107, 148–149, 152, 169–170, 205
decreed, 80, 95, 129, 168
decretive, 130, 132
depraved, 14, 26, 48, 102, 124, 170
depravity, 16, 27, 29, 31, 33, 35, 37, 39, 41, 43–45, 47–59, 61–63, 65, 71–72, 99, 101, 104, 106, 111–112, 124, 134, 137, 139
determination, 22, 77, 86, 115, 129, 132–133, 148
determinism, 66–69, 82–83, 85–86, 97, 183
deterministic, 82, 86, 181, 183
Deuteronomy, 49, 145
devil, 6, 33, 55, 59
dishonor, 179
dishonorable, 179
disobedience, 5, 7, 38, 41
disobedient, 130
disobey, 32, 130
Dordrecht, 27
dort, 17, 24, 27–29, 42, 55, 59, 114, 167, 194

E

eastern, 32

Index

Ecclesiastes, 48
ecumenical, 12
ecumenically, 6
Eden, 32
edicts, 182
effectual, 113–114, 116–119, 122–124, 133, 136
effectually, 99, 112, 114, 119, 133–134, 168, 195, 202, 204
efficacious, 79, 113, 132, 137
efficaciously, 79, 117, 196
effort, 16, 100, 177
Egypt, 89, 92, 179
election, 2, 8, 22, 25, 27, 29, 68–69, 82, 97, 114, 127, 135, 142–153, 155, 157–169, 171, 173–181, 183, 185, 196, 204, 209
enablement, 17, 104–105, 125
enlightening, 114, 181
enslaved, 6, 15, 26, 50
Ephesians, 33, 49, 129, 135, 148, 151, 157–158, 166, 174, 183, 196
Ephesus, 6, 32
Essene, 69
eternal, 13, 33, 42, 44, 56, 60, 62, 93, 102, 109, 118, 121, 129, 147, 149, 152, 155–156, 166–167, 169, 174, 187, 192, 201–204, 206, 209–211, 213
eternally, 129, 202, 204–205
eternity, 81, 129, 155–156, 165, 168, 195
evangelical, 101, 103, 132, 138, 147, 216
eve, 6, 32–34, 42, 45, 57, 60
exodus, 74, 131

F
faith, 2–3, 8, 13–14, 16, 25–26, 29, 36, 42–44, 51–52, 54, 56, 60, 72, 84, 87, 99, 101–103, 106, 111–112, 114, 118–120, 126–127, 133–137, 139–142, 150, 152–156, 158–169, 171, 173, 178, 185, 188, 192–195, 197, 202–213, 217
faithful, 16, 78, 145, 183
faithfully, 66, 195
fatalism, 86
fatalists, 18
firstborn, 154, 171
foreknew, 96, 117, 154–156, 158, 166, 171, 191, 202
foreknow, 95, 148, 155–156, 172
foreknowledge, 2, 66, 75–76, 80–82, 87, 94–96, 117, 120, 136, 143, 150, 152,

Index

154–155, 161, 173
foreknown, 92, 95, 112, 114, 152–153, 155, 172
foreloves, 173
foreloving, 154–155, 171
forensic, 212
foreordain, 145
foreordained, 80, 95, 168
foreordaines, 130
foreordination, 80, 95–96, 154, 171
foresight, 154–155, 171
forgiveness, 3, 118, 157, 211
freedom, 3, 6–7, 12–13, 17, 19, 24, 49, 57–58, 66–67, 69, 71–74, 77–78, 82–84, 86, 88–90, 94, 97, 106, 115, 124, 128, 133, 177–179, 184, 209
freely, 6, 26, 49, 81, 84, 87, 92, 94, 114, 168
freewill, 181, 204
fruit, 60, 206–207, 213

G

Galatians, 160, 177, 195
generation, 21, 42–43, 55, 60
Genesis, 32–33, 48, 89, 92, 130, 145, 177
geneva, 21
gentile, 125, 147, 162
gift, 8, 13, 15, 26, 38, 41, 106, 112, 127, 135, 141, 152, 167, 194, 203–205, 207
glorification, 117, 133, 142, 173, 202, 204, 213
glorified, 117, 133, 147, 154, 156, 169, 171–173, 180, 202–203, 208
glory, 33, 44, 49, 133, 150, 168, 179–180, 195, 217
Gomarus, 25
gracious, 16, 105, 111, 116, 131, 136, 162, 165, 194
graciously, 107, 167
guilt, 5, 31–37, 39–40, 42–47, 54, 60, 79, 140, 189

H

headship, 42, 45–46
Heaven, 108–109, 131, 144, 150, 157, 175, 202
Hebrew, 145
Heidelberg, 24–25, 44, 54, 189
heir, 176

Index

heresy, 12, 27, 188
holiness, 44, 167, 205–206
humanity, 6, 13–14, 34, 48, 51, 60, 62, 73, 102, 104, 137
humankind, 96, 147, 182
humans, 5–6, 32, 47, 63, 75, 77, 84, 90, 94, 133, 162

I

imputation, 34, 36–37, 42, 45–46, 188–189
imputed, 36, 42–43, 45, 60, 211
inability, 16, 53, 56, 58, 65, 137
incarnate, 6, 33, 147
inclination, 13, 32–33, 63, 137
inclined, 6, 20, 32, 49, 56, 59
incoherent, 117
incompatibilism, 61, 66–67, 90, 97
incompatibilist, 93
infralapsarianism, 21–22, 25
inherently, 18, 32
inherit, 5, 33, 41, 46, 144
inherited, 5, 33, 36
initiation, 16, 26
initiative, 15, 101, 145, 172
injustice, 161, 178
invitation, 108, 118–120
irresistible, 15, 17–18, 29, 99, 101, 108, 110–111, 113, 120, 122, 124, 133–134, 141
irresistibly, 210
Isaac, 160, 176–177
Isaiah, 92, 129
Iscariot, 92
Ishmael, 160, 177
Israel, 92, 132, 145, 147, 160–162, 175–177
Israelites, 131, 161, 183

J

Jacob, 21, 23, 44–45, 53, 71, 77, 79, 101, 154, 160–161, 176–177, 189
Jeremiah, 33, 48–49
Jerusalem, 74, 107, 131, 197

Index

jew, 125, 160, 162, 175
John, 21, 34, 48, 58, 74, 83, 92, 101–102, 108–111, 116, 120, 124–125, 137–138, 140, 146, 191–192, 197–198, 202–203, 207
Joseph, 72, 89, 91–92, 94, 109
Josephus, 68–69
Joshua, 74
Judaism, 68, 181, 183
judas, 92–93, 146
Judea, 197
judgment, 38, 41, 59, 118, 167, 180
judicial, 43
justice, 161, 166, 169, 178, 189, 210
justification, 19–20, 36, 38, 41, 45, 117, 140–142, 168, 183, 189, 204, 211–213

L

libertarian, 67–69, 71–75, 78, 82, 88, 90, 93–94, 106, 124, 128, 133, 209
libertarianism, 67–69, 75, 82–84, 89–90, 97, 99
luke, 92, 95, 108, 119, 131, 145–146, 166, 198
Luther, 19–21
Lutheran, 10, 76
Lutheranism, 9, 18

M

Matthew, 10, 24, 44, 48, 53, 56, 71, 74, 92, 104, 107, 119, 131, 149–150, 189, 207, 209, 211
mediator, 146–147, 168
medieval, 21
Melanchthon, 10, 19
mercied, 178
merciful, 167
mercy, 7, 45, 118, 128, 133, 161–165, 168–170, 178–180, 189
merit, 6, 10, 42, 57, 158, 204
messiah, 162, 164, 175
methodist, 56
Molinism, 76
monergism, 7, 9, 137
monergistic, 3, 9–10
monergists, 137

Index

morally, 74, 85, 103
mortality, 33, 36
Moses, 37, 55, 131, 145, 161, 192
motivations, 72, 94
motive, 49

N
Netherlands, 27, 216

O
omnipotent, 76
omniscience, 80
omniscient, 127, 155
orthodox, 32, 34, 55, 151
orthodoxy, 32

P
paganism, 3
parable, 108, 119–120
Paul, 34, 38, 40, 42, 49–52, 69, 87, 94, 116–117, 122, 125, 146–147, 151, 159–164, 166, 172, 175–181, 183–184, 202–203
Pauline, 68–69
pelagian, 1–3, 11–12, 14, 17–20, 26, 36, 71
pelagianism, 1–3, 5, 9, 11–12, 15–20, 58, 215
pelagius, 5–6, 12–13, 32, 42
Pentecost, 93
perish, 74, 121–122, 192, 203
permission, 78, 88–89
perseverance, 8, 27, 29, 201–207, 209–211, 213
persevere, 202, 204–207, 209, 213
persons, 105, 118, 129, 132, 144, 151, 168
persuasion, 105, 127
persuasive, 26
Peter, 74, 95, 116, 124, 126, 128, 132, 146, 172, 180, 192, 197, 212
pharaoh, 92, 131, 162, 164, 179–180
pharisee, 69, 181, 184
Philip, 19
Philippians, 38, 135, 177, 202

Index

pilate, 93
polytheism, 3
posterity, 42–45, 55, 60
potter, 162, 164, 179, 182
powerfully, 88, 114, 168, 195
prayer, 13
predestinarian, 69, 183
predestinated, 114, 147, 166, 174
predestination, 2, 8, 14–16, 24, 65–66, 68–69, 82, 96, 117, 120, 143, 145, 147–155, 157, 159, 161, 163, 165, 167, 169–171, 173, 175, 177, 179, 181, 183, 185, 187, 196, 199
predestine, 148
predestined, 95, 117, 120, 151–152, 154–157, 166, 171–172, 174, 185, 202, 208
predestining, 8, 117, 151, 173
predetermined, 80–81
predetermines, 150
prescience, 154–155, 171
preservation, 121, 202, 204–205, 207, 209
prevenient, 7, 15–16, 20, 26–27, 62, 99, 101–106, 111–113, 123–126, 133–134, 136, 142, 191
priest, 189
priesthood, 145
priestly, 189
prophets, 107, 109, 131, 207
propitiation, 45, 192
propitiatory, 189
Proverbs, 49, 91
Providence, 69, 77, 87, 181
providential, 78, 85, 89–90
provision, 191

Q
qualification, 170

R
realism, 34
rebel, 85
rebelling, 59

Index

rebellion, 32, 115
rebrobate, 152
redeemer, 203, 216
redemption, 4, 16, 26, 107, 117, 157, 160, 164, 168, 189, 203
redemptive, 160
reform, 60
reformation, 17, 19–20, 24, 144
reformed, 10, 12, 15–17, 21–22, 24–25, 27–28, 40, 43–44, 53–54, 104, 136, 189, 194, 203, 206, 208, 210–212, 216
reformers, 21
regenerate, 8, 139, 205
restored, 9, 139
regenerating, 102, 114, 136
regeneration, 3, 7, 10, 60, 102, 115, 135–142, 204
rejection, 62, 107, 123, 134, 147, 160–161, 164, 188
relational, 105
relationship, 31, 33, 42, 47, 63, 68, 96, 116, 125, 132, 137, 145, 172–173, 183, 196
remnant, 145, 176–177, 183
remonstrance, 17, 24, 26–27, 55, 189
remonstrant, 101
renouncing, 211–212
repent, 100–101, 108, 124, 137, 164, 212
repentance, 24, 74, 118, 178, 192, 211
repentant, 20
repented, 212
reprobate, 112, 151, 169
reprobation, 22–23, 25, 152, 159–160, 167, 169–170
reprobative, 151
resistance, 74, 111, 115
resistible, 12, 27, 72, 97, 99, 101, 106–107, 117, 120, 122–123, 133, 141
response, 9, 16–17, 20, 25, 105, 114, 117, 122, 127, 136, 138, 148, 159, 164, 174, 179, 189, 206
responsibility, 2, 31, 67, 73, 85–87, 94, 111, 117–118, 130, 181
restoration, 115
resurrection, 33, 217
revelation, 95, 104–105, 112, 118
revival, 17, 21
revives, 115

Index

righteous, 38, 41–43, 50–51, 88, 167, 209
righteousness, 36–38, 41–45, 51–52, 56–59, 138, 159, 188–189, 209, 211, 215
Romans, 24, 33, 37–38, 40, 43–45, 49–52, 58, 117, 125, 148, 154, 158–159, 162–163, 170–172, 175, 177, 180–181, 183, 202

S

Sadducees, 69
saint, 202
salvation, 2–4, 6, 8, 10, 13–17, 19, 22, 25–26, 32–33, 42, 47, 56–57, 71, 85, 96, 101–103, 105, 107, 111, 114, 117–118, 126, 128–129, 131–133, 135–137, 140, 142, 144–146, 148–150, 152–153, 156, 159–165, 167–170, 172, 176, 178–179, 185, 190–192, 194–195, 197, 201, 203, 206, 208–210, 213, 215, 217
salvific, 100, 104, 117, 120, 155, 178
sanctification, 140, 142, 168, 205
sanctified, 183, 202, 204
sanctifying, 140
satan, 56, 92, 204
satisfaction, 43, 189, 194
savable, 124
savingly, 114
savior, 22, 111, 192, 197
Shepherd, 120–122, 197
sinful, 3, 5, 7, 14, 32–33, 47–49, 57–58, 60, 62–63, 65, 79, 87–89, 101–102
sinfulness, 48, 51, 88, 137, 189
sinner, 7, 15, 19, 26, 45, 48, 74, 100, 110, 116, 136, 155, 163, 183
Sira, 68, 182
Sirach, 181–183
soteriology, 2–3, 9, 82
souls, 168
sovereign, 76–77, 85–86, 91, 132–133, 148, 164, 168, 179, 182, 194
sovereignly, 120
sovereignty, 2, 20, 62, 65–66, 68, 74–77, 82, 85–87, 90–91, 93–94, 97, 130, 146, 161, 178–182, 184
spiritual, 13, 20, 32–33, 49, 56, 59–60, 63, 85, 100, 102, 115, 125, 136–137, 140, 158
spiritually, 49, 56, 114–115
Sproul, 17, 136, 141
Spurgeon, 196, 206

Index

Stephen, 104
supernatural, 14, 104
supralapsarian, 22, 25
supralapsarianism, 21–22, 25, 170
synergism, 7, 9–10, 12, 14, 16
synergist, 10–11
synergistic, 4, 9–13, 15, 26
synod, 14–17, 27, 55

T
temple, 68–69, 181, 183
temporal, 8, 21, 44, 60, 139, 205
theodicy, 75
theory, 94, 188
Thessalonians, 179
Thomas, 10, 125, 138
Timothy, 48, 56, 75, 122, 132, 167, 180, 197
Titus, 102
tradition, 12, 17, 26, 28, 32, 36, 40, 90, 97, 113, 141, 151, 194, 196, 206, 208
transgress, 163
transgressing, 163
transgression, 5, 32, 37, 41, 60

U
unbelief, 122, 127, 192
unbeliever, 211
unbelieving, 161, 164, 191
unconditional, 25, 29, 114, 142–143, 148–150, 153, 156, 158–159, 161–162, 165–166, 174–175, 178, 185
unconditionally, 159, 178, 210
universalism, 132, 188, 192
universalists, 188
unmerited, 102, 145
unregenerate, 8, 55, 119
unrighteousness, 32
unwilling, 107, 115
unwillingness, 107–108

Index

W
Wesley, 124
Wesleyan, 16, 56, 112, 189
Westminster, 29, 42–43, 60, 114, 202, 204–205
willfully, 133–134, 163
willingly, 79, 100, 113, 116, 133–134
wisdom, 68, 87, 103, 157, 181
wolves, 197
wrath, 7, 33, 40, 43–44, 59–60, 133, 163–164, 179, 189

Z
Zwingli, 34

Printed by Amazon Italia Logistica S.r.l.
Torrazza Piemonte (TO), Italy

65175075R00178